THE ORIGINAL MICHAEL FRAYN

The Original Michael Frayn

SATIRICAL ESSAYS BY
MICHAEL FRAYN
CHOSEN AND INTRODUCED BY
JAMES FENTON

1983
The Salamander Press
Edinburgh

The Salamander Press Edinburgh Ltd
34 Shandwick Place, Edinburgh, EH2 4RT
This selection first published October 1983
ISBN 0 907540 32 5 (*hardback*)
ISBN 0 907540 33 3 (*paperback*)

Printed and made in Great Britain
Set in VIP Garamond
by Fakenham Photosetting Ltd, Fakenham, Norfolk.
Printed by Spottiswoode Ballantyne Ltd, Colchester, Essex.
Designed and edited by Tom Fenton at the Salamander Press.

ACKNOWLEDGEMENTS

The first twenty pieces in this collection were originally published, between 1960 and 1962, in *The Guardian*, and are reproduced here by permission of the Editor. They were subsequently reissued in two collections, *The Day of the Dog* (1962) and *The Book of Fub* (1963), both published by Collins.

The remaining pieces were originally published, between 1962 and 1968, in *The Observer*, and are reproduced here by permission of the Editor. The first twelve of these were reissued in *On the Outskirts* (Collins 1964); the following 23 in *At Bay in Gear Street* (Fontana 1967). The last nineteen *Observer* pieces, all written in 1967 and 1968, have not previously been collected.

Contents

Introduction   *page* 9

from *The Day of the Dog* (1962)

Strain Cook Thoroughly Before Serving   13
I Think I'm Right in Saying   15
Lady with Polythenias   17
Twelfth Night; or, What Will You Have?   19
Behind the Myth—Mythtier Thtill   21
Every Day in Every Way   23
Gagg Speaks   25
Plain Speaking on S'Agaro   28

from *The Book of Fub* (1963)

Housebiz   30
The Great Shikar of 1896   32
Never Put Off to Gomorrah   34
Listener Sport   36
Chez Crumble   38
Bodbury: The Nation Waits   41
Bodbury Speaks Out!   43
The Sunshine Life   45
D. Op.   47
A Letter from the Publisher   49
Lloyd   51
From the Improved Version   54

from *On The Outskirts* (1964)

I Said, "My Name is 'Ozzy' Manders, Dean of King's"   56
And Home's Son's Father is Hume's Father's Son   58
Ron Number   61
The Sad Tale of P-t-r B-nnykin   64

Fog-like Sensations 67
Dig My Dogma 69
The Mails Must Go Through 72
Oh, Un Peu, Vous Savez, Un Peu 74
Total Scholarship 77
What the Peepers See 79
On the Subject of Objects 82
Divine News, Darlings! 85

from *At Bay in Gear Street* (1967)

A Question of Downbringing 87
The Monolithic View of Mirrors 90
Inside the Krankenhaus 92
The Meteorological School 95
Firm Friends of Ours 98
Substance Without Soul 100
Business Worries 103
Childholders 106
My Nature Diary 109
Lives and Likenesses 112
School of Applied Art 114
The Normal Fifth 117
The Battle of the Books 120
Between the Acts 122
H.I.5 125
Hommes de Plume 128
Tête-à-Tête-à-Tête 131
Ivan Kudovbin 133
Cottage Industry 136
Spock's Guide to Parent Care 139
What the Mice Foretell 141
Return Match 144
At Bay in Gear Street 147

Uncollected Pieces

Can You Hear Me, Mother? 150
On The Receiving End 153
A Hand of Cards 156
With All The Stops Out 160

Child and Superchild 162
In the Morris Manner 165
Pas Devant les Enfants 168
A Princess in Disguise 171
Facing the Music 173
57 Types of Ambiguity 176
In the Superurbs 179
H & C 182
A Question of Character 185
A Wisp of Azure 187
What the Stars Foretell 190
East of Suez 193
Private Collections 195
Save it for the Stairs 198
A Very Special Collection 201

Introduction

As far as I can tell from hanging around in all the likely secondhand bookshops, those people who bought Michael Frayn's classic collections of humorous pieces are not inclined to part with them. They will chuck out the Longfellow, they will flog off Mrs Hemans, and vast numbers of them appear to have got rid of Clochemerle as soon as they read it. If you check the humour shelves you will find plenty of what you don't want—Oliver Wendel Holmes, say, or Alpha of the Plough. But *The Day of the Dog*, *The Book of Fub*, *On the Outskirts* and *At Bay in Gear Street*—signed or unsigned, foxed or unfoxed, with or without original wrappers—you may as well whistle for them.

I imagine that when the marriages of *Guardian* and *Observer* readers broke up at the end of the Sixties, there was an awkward moment when it came to dividing up the Frayn collection. As *his* fingers paused over *Fub*, *she* could be heard indulging that significant cough: "*Actually*, that was a present to *me*, darling. You remember, surely." Or as *she* was changing the locks, *he* was consulting his solicitors over the restitution of certain property. Hang the children, and never mind the lovingly restored cottage with its bright kitchen paintwork, enamel mugs and frayed rush-matting squares. What really mattered was the loss of *At Bay*.

A further circumstance may have helped to render these books unobtainable—their value as a source of comic ideas for later, less original writers. The attentive reader will find here many a promising trope on its first outing, and many a journalist may be obliged to blush and exclaim, "Oh I'd *completely forgotten* that one . . . I could have sworn *I* invented it." But I am afraid that, innocently or not, we have pilfered much from Michael Frayn, and it's time we returned what we snitched.

In order to make this selection, I was obliged to borrow such copies as the author still had in his collection, and supplement this with a rare Hampstead quarto of *At Bay*, unavailable in the Stiftung Frayn. The author also kindly supplied xeroxes of uncollected *Observer* pieces, checked the selection, made the odd excision and suggested one or two items which people are always trying to track down. The result, I hope will reasonably satisfy most of the old fans, and bring new readers to a source of much laughter.

Those *Observer* xeroxes came with a handy guide to the spirit of the age, in the form of the "Sayings of the Week", which used to be tucked inside the articles. Thus, on one page we find an aged (but by no means dying) General Franco announcing: "If those who are talking about a contrast of opinions are in fact searching for political parties, let them know that it will never occur." Later, Mr Nicholas Katzenbach, the US Under Secretary of State, can be heard (and how clearly this voice travels) protesting: "It would not correctly reflect our limited motives in Vietnam to use outmoded phraseology ... a declaration of war."

Elsewhere Miss Jennie Lee asserts that she would rather be handed a flower than have an atom bomb thrown at her, a worried Dubcek warns that in a socialist democracy the leading role of the party must not be weakened, and a certain Lord Huntly remarks: "One day, before I die, something may arouse me to such an extent that I shall be forced to go and speak in the House."

This is recognisably our world, but it is no longer quite the same. Franco turned out to be mortal and wrong. The theatre of undeclared war has shifted. Miss Lee became a baroness and perhaps—who knows?—even bumped into Lord Huntly, who perhaps was even moved to open his mouth in the House. In the same way, the world which Michael Frayn evokes, in the course of articles written between 1959 and 1968, is recognisably ours, and yet also has acquired a certain patina or period flavour. One can see, for instance, that Christopher Smoothe, MP, would have had a responsible position in the Heath Government. But it is by no means certain that his career would be flourishing under Thatcher—for the simple reason that there are too many other Christopher Smoothes jockeying for position.

Fashions in humour may have changed since the 1960s, but I cannot believe that the humour itself of these pieces will appear dated. Michael Frayn's virtues as a comic writer were always based on an ability to evoke the instantly recognisable—the awful predicament, the common foible, the typical character. He is the funniest journalist of our time, and he is also *the* master of comic form. These are not merely sustained jokes. They are model essays.

After the form had lost its attraction, Michael Frayn turned to fiction and plays. It is, to the outsider, a very satisfyingly shaped career—precisely the same career (minus the TB) as Chekhov. I shan't push the comparison, I merely wish to point out that admirers of Frayn the playwright may be curious to see how the original Michael Frayn developed his craft. But for most people, of course, the sufficient reason for reading this collection is that, from now on, you are not going to be able to keep a straight face.

JAMES FENTON
Oxford, July 1983

Strain Cook Thoroughly Before Serving

When I was a bachelor I used to dine variously on fried eggs, fried bacon, fried eggs and fried bacon, or fried bacon and fried eggs. There were also occasional days when I had forgotten to buy either eggs or bacon.

My somewhat limited range in the culinary field has earned me but a menial position in the kitchen now that I am married. I am allowed to peel the potatoes and empty the trashcan, provided I stand to attention when spoken to, but not to prod the soufflés, or baste the beans, or whatever real cooks do.

There are, however, certain recipes which reduce my wife to such a state of nervous disintegration that she is forced to lean on me abjectly. I mean the sort written by authors who haven't yet heard the good news about the invention of weights and measures. And if a recipe-writer still hasn't got round to the concept of ounces and pints (or for that matter hins and cubic cubits—we're prepared to make every effort to compromise), you can bet your bottom tealeaf that he hasn't managed to grasp the principles of written communication either, or of predicting what tools and materials he is going to need until he has actually picked them up.

I hear despairing cries from the kitchen, and find my wife set on making a recipe which starts off: "Pour a fair amount of milk into a medium-sized bowl, and throw in a generous handful of soya beans. Add a modicum of grated cheese and the quantity of chopped chives which will lie on a sovereign piece."

I help my wife choose a particularly medium-sized looking bowl, and supply the generosity for measuring out the soya beans. "Take a few eggs," the recipe goes on, "and carefully separate the whites from the yolks. Now whisk them into the mixture." The whites or the yolks? We compromise with a half of each.

13

"Fry the mixture for a few minutes over a hottish flame, until it is the colour of a walnut sideboard, and there is black edging round the shredded onion." The shredded onion? "This should have been added before the soya beans in order to prevent the milk curdling. Now quickly transfer the mixture to a cast-zinc stew-pan."

"Run out to the corner," shouts my wife, "and buy a cast-zinc stew-pan." I run all the way there and back. "You'll have to go out again," she cries on my return. "After I've transferred the mixture to the cast-zinc stew-pan I've got to add a very large eggcupful of icing-sugar." Without a word of protest I run all the way back to the corner and get the icing-sugar. "No, no, no!" shouts my wife as I stumble breathlessly back into the kitchen with it. "I've got the icing-sugar—I wanted you to buy the very large eggcup."

When I stagger painfully back into the room again with the eggcup, I find my wife sieving tiny pieces of raw meat out of the mixture. "The recipe," she sobs, "says: 'Pour the mixture over a jam-jarful of minced beef.'"

"Then why are you taking the beef out again?"

"The next sentence says: 'The beef should have been roasted for an hour first.'"

We force-roast the beef, and brace ourselves for what lies ahead. "Place an asbestos mat beneath the dish," says the recipe, "and beat it with a wooden spoon. Continue beating until, at the bottom, the top of it is covered underneath with a grey sauce of sodden soya bean. The bottom of it should then rise out of it, coming through the top of it (the pan) until the rest of it (the bottom of it) can be separated from it, and placed in a pie-dish beaten to the consistency of thin gruel. Bake briskly. When a fine blue aromatic smoke begins to rise, the mixture is hopelessly overcooked."

It is quite late at night when the fine blue aromatic smoke at last curls out of the oven, and we are both very tired and weak with hunger. My wife turns over the page and reads the last sentence of the recipe: "Before serving, store in a cool place for at least a fortnight to allow fermentation to finish."

Well, well. But the canned luncheon meat, I must admit, is opened to a turn.

14

I Think I'm Right in Saying

Orators of any standing no longer orate, and it's a pretty third-rate writer nowadays who is reduced to writing. These antique forms of communication have been replaced by the interview. Would you agree, Mr. Frayn?

—Oh yes, entirely.

I believe I'm right in saying that you yourself have given up writing, Mr. Frayn, and have instead put yourself in the hands of a competent interviewer. Tell me, is this forward-looking move aimed at easing the strain of thinking, or is it purely an attempt to gain status?

—A bit of both, I think.

I wonder if you agree with me that this technique is capable of considerable extension? It seems to me demeaning in the extreme for Lord Mayors and others to be forced back on the monologue form at ceremonial occasions. It would surely add tone and dignity to the occasion if a good interviewer asked the Lord Mayor:

"What does it give you, sir, to be present here today?"

"Very great pleasure," the Lord Mayor would reply.

"And what organ is this good cause very close to?"

"My heart."

"I see. But I believe you're sure that people haven't come here to do one thing?"

"To listen to me talking."

"So what do you intend to proceed without?"

"Any further ado."

"One last question, sir. What do you declare this home for asthmatic engine-drivers?"

"Open."

What do you think of these proposals, Mr. Frayn?

—Oh, admirable.

I feel (perhaps you will agree with me) that the whole course of human history would have had much more tone and class if these techniques had been put into practice earlier.

—Yes, I suppose so.

I was thinking, for instance, of the rather tedious monologue which Mark Antony delivered to the crowd in the Forum. How much more satisfactory it would have been if some well-informed commentator had introduced him.

"Friends, Romans, countrymen," he might have started off, "lend that well-known personality, Mark Antony, your ears. Mr. Antony, it's a great honour to have you with us here in the Forum. What exactly is the purpose of your visit?"

"I come to bury Caesar," Antony would reply.

"Not to praise him?"

"Definitely not."

"Mr. Antony, you've been quoted in some of the Londinium papers as saying that the evil that men do is oft interred with their bones. Would you care to comment on this?"

"I'm afraid they've got hold of the wrong end of the stick entirely. What I actually said was that the evil that men do lives after them. It was the good, I said, which was oft interred with their bones."

"And your attitude is, if I may put words into your mouth, 'So let it be with Caesar'?"

"Exactly."

The mob would have remained completely calm and orderly under these circumstances, don't you think, Mr. Frayn?

—What? Oh, yes.

Do you think the technique could also be used in the parliamentary and political fields? Would it add interest and variety to speeches that of necessity contain lists of proposals? For instance, I can imagine a good political journalist helping out with:

"Welcome back to the dispatch box, Mr. Churchill. I think the question that's uppermost in all our minds tonight is what you, as Prime Minister, have to offer the English people."

"Nothing but blood and sweat."

"Nothing else at all?"

"I'm afraid not."

"How about tears?"

"Oh well, yes, some tears, if you like."

16

The same man could have done wonders at the Labour Party Conference at Scarborough.

"What do you propose to do, Mr. Gaitskell? Fight or not?"

"Oh, rather."

"Which, fight?"

"I beg your pardon?"

"I said 'fight' again."

"Oh, again and again and again."

Well, thank you, Mr. Frayn, for coming along and answering my questions so frankly.

—As a matter of fact, Mr. Frayn's gone to bed, suffering from creative exhaustion. I'm the interviewer who's come to interview *you*. Perhaps you'd care to start off by telling us all what it's like to be a famous interviewer. . . .

Lady with Polythenias

Viscountess Scarsdale recently advertised for someone to darn her husband's socks, and, if reports in my favourite gossip column are correct, evinced what might be described as indignation on receiving several rather rude answers. "People seem to imagine," she cried, "one lies around all day on a chaise-longue simply devouring chocolates. Quite absurd."

Only too, too wrong in fact, for it seems that a viscountess's work is never done. In Lady Scarsdale's case this is scarcely surprising, for she says it takes her two hours each day to do the flowers. She then sometimes has to struggle through the veritable floral jungle this must have created to find Newton the butler and help him mend the carpets with "some stuff we buy at Woolworths."

Well, I have good news for Lady Scarsdale. It is of a labour-saving device which will enable her to devote two hours a day to her husband's socks, or one hour to the socks and one hour to devouring chocolates on the chaise-longue, whichever she feels to be her duty. Woolworths, the old family firm who have been supplying carpet-mending materials man and boy to the

Scarsdales of Kedleston ever since the carpets first needed mending, can now also supply plastic flowers.

Hardened as I am to the swift march of progress, I must admit that I felt a certain shock when I looked into my local branch of Woolworths the other day for a fresh supply of carpet-mending materials and saw a counter loaded with plastic flowers. I picked up the pamphlet which went with them and read: "The loveliness of real flowers authentically reproduced in the magic of polythene, the new wonder plastic! . . . use them indoors—use them in window-boxes—plant them in the garden where you need an extra patch of colour! They're durable, washable, waterproof, and weatherproof . . . strew them as decorations on your dinner-table, making, in the light of your electric candles, a pretty picture of elegance and luxury."

It's the electric candles that convince me. Woolworths are introducing us not only to plastic flowers, but to a whole new way of life. Let's take the case of Lady Bagshot. Once upon a time Lady Bagshot had to slave all day over a hot flower-pot to keep Bagshot Hall, the Bagshots' little semi-detached castle, looking nice. Her husband's socks consequently fell into such a terrible state of disrepair that not even his best friends cared to be seen out with him, and the Bagshots' marriage seemed to be heading for disaster . . . until one day Lady Bagshot discovered Woolworths.

Three months later we find her in the West Drawing Room at Bagshot Hall amid a scene of indescribable elegance and luxury. The great room is lit by a hundred flickering electric candles, whose soft glow falls on banked masses of polythene roses, nylon delphiniums, and rayon azaleas. Lady Bagshot herself is reclining on a plastic chaise-longue, sticking Scotch tape over the holes in a pair of "Terylene" socks, and gracefully devouring synthetic peppermint creams.

There is a trampling noise from somewhere among the rot-proof plastic azaleas, and eventually Lord Bagshot emerges, home from a hard day's hunting.

Lady B.: Had a good day, darling?

Lord B.: Not bad. The M.F.H. got rather a bad shock off the electric fox, but my horse is going like a bomb now we've got that new high-compression head on the cylinder-block. How about you?

Lady B.: I've been very busy. Now that we've replanted the whole estate with plastic flora it only takes me half an hour to pick the flowers for the house each morning, and no time at all to pop them in the artificial water. At last I've really got a chance to get down to some serious synthetic-chocolate eating. I managed to get through four pounds of them today.

Lord B.: Good work, old thing.

Lady B.: And, darling, I've got a little secret to tell you too. (*She blushes modestly and lowers her eyes.*) I wasn't sure at first ... but I know how much you've always wanted an heir....

Lord B.: I say, old girl! You don't mean ...?

Lady B.: Yes!

Lord B.: But how simply splendid! When's it going to be?

Lady B.: Just as soon as I can get into Woolworths to collect it.

(*She lifts her radiant face to his, so that her contact lenses shine in the electric candlelight.*)

Oh, think, Baggy, our very own plastic baby!

Twelfth Night; or, What Will You Have?

The other day my wife bought a jar of what were described on the label as "Old English Cocktail Olives." Ah, evocative words! They bring vividly to mind that golden age when England was still covered with primeval olive groves and when the rip-roaring Old English Cocktail Party was in full flower. ·Like most Old English things, it was at its best in Elizabethan times—to judge, at any rate, from the following fragment, entitled *Ye Cocktayle Partye*, and attributed to Will Shakespeare (by Mike Frayn, at any rate).

(*Scene: The Earl of Essex's At Home.*)

Essex: Ah, good Northumberland! Thou com'st betimes! What drink'st? Martini? Champagne cup? Or hock?

Or that wan distillate whose fiery soul
Is tamed by th' hailstones hurl'd from jealous heaven,
The draught a breed of men yet unengender'd
Calls Scotch on th' rocks?
Northumberland: Ay, Scotch, but stint the rocks.
Essex: Ah, Gloucester! And your fairest Duchess, too!
Sweet Leicester! Ah, my Lady Leicester, homage!
And Worcester, and the Chesters, radiant pair!
And Ursula, the sister of Lord Bicester!
Northumberland, methinks thou know'st not Gloucester,
Nor Gloucester Worcester, nor the Leicesters Chesters.
Lord Worcester, may I introduce Lord Leicester?
My noblest Gloucester, meet your brother Chester.
My Lady Chester and my Lady Leicester,
Meet Ursula, the sister of Lord Bicester.
All: Hail!
Gloucester: Well, now, hath Phoebus quit these climes for ever?
Worcester: Ay, are we now delivered quite to gales,
And spouting hurricanoes' plashy spite?
Chester: Sure, 'tis foul weather.
Leicester: Why, so 'tis.
Northumberland: 'Tis so.
(Another part of the battlefield.)
Essex: What ho, champagne! Crisps, ho! Pass round the
peanuts!
Worcester: A peanut, madam? Pardon me, I pray,
But when we met, the white-hot dazzlement
Your beauty rains about like thunderbolts
Quite seared my eyes; I did not catch your name.
Lady Ursula: Why, Ursula, and sister to Lord Bicester.
Worcester: Not Harry Bicester? Known to th' admiring
world
As Eggy? Wears a red moustache?
Ursula: The same.
Worcester: O, Eggy Bicester! and thou, thou art his sister?
Then long-lost cousins must we surely be!
Essex: Forgive me, Ursula, if I intrude,
But, Worcester, meet our brother Chester here.
He has the royal birthmark on his arm,
Would know if you had, too.

Worcester: Why, so I have.
Chester: Why, marry then, you are my brother, stol'n
  At birth by she-bears.
Worcester: Why then, that I am!
Lady Leicester: The truth of th' ancient legend now is clear:
  "When Worcester linkt to Chester prove to be,
  "Then Gloucester in Northumberland we'll see."
  Northumberland is Gloucester, chang'd at birth,
  And Gloucester Worcester, while the aged Earl
  Of Leicester plainly must be Lady Chester,
  All chang'd, and double-chang'd, and chang'd again,
  The Chesters Leicesters and the Leicesters Chesters,
  Lord Chester, thus, the proof runs clear, is me,
  And Ursula, Lord Bicester, his own sister.
Northumberland: Before the discourse turns again to weigh
  Apollo's absence and the pluvious times,
  We should acquaint our new selves with each other.
  My Lady Chester, once the Earl of Leicester,
  Meet Lady Leicester, now the Earl of Chester....
Essex: Old friends 'neath curious titles oft are found;
  Come, pass th' Old English Cocktail Olives round....

Behind the Myth—Mythtier Thtill

You ring the bell, and when the door opens you walk inside.
"I'm afraid Mr. Tramplin's still in the bath," says someone.
You note the remark down. You've come to do a cultural
interview for a highbrow publication, and you have a lot of
space to fill. You sit down to wait in a respectful attitude. You
assume your readers will guess that when you say you you
mean not they but I.

You just have time to glance round the room and notice a
calendar, a set of telephone directories, and several ashtrays,
before Victor Tramplin comes in. He apologises modestly for
keeping you waiting. To hear him you would scarcely think he
was one of the great old personalities of the cinema. It seems

21

incredible that this quiet, modest man has been playing the front legs of film monsters for so long that he has become accepted by intellectual *cinéastes* as a front legs of profound natural integrity.

"Mr. Tramplin," you say, "over a career which has included such rôles as the front legs of the pterodactyl in *It came from Prehistoric Space*, the front legs of the fly in *The Monster Fly*, and the front legs of the giant bat in *Secrets of the Horror Crypt*, you have become accepted by intellectual *cinéastes* as a front legs of profound natural integrity."

"Yes," he replies, and you begin to see a new side to his character you hadn't suspected before, the man of action hacking his way through the jungle of cultural verbiage with a decisive monosyllable.

"Mr. Tramplin," you go on, "may I ask you a very personal question? What do you think about the place of the artist in society?"

He doesn't answer at once. He looks at you with something like puzzlement in his eyes, almost blankly, and you realise that here is another aspect of Tramplin the front legs—the plain man facing up to the immense question-marks of our times and not letting himself be rushed. "What do I think about the place of the artist in society?" he repeats, and it is a blow struck for the plain man everywhere against the tyranny of his inquisitors. "Why, I think he's got a damn' nice little place out there."

You write it down. This is another side to the man. The plain citizen defending himself against the jargon of the experts can also become the expert himself uttering the calm inscrutable wisdom of the oracle.

Suddenly he laughs and you realise it was all a joke—a wry, self-depreciatory comment, turning, he explains, on the double meaning of "place."

This is yet another Tramplin—Tramplin the eternal clown, mocking the world from the sawdust ring of his soul. "Sorry for the gag," he says, and his sorrow—the pathos of the clown behind the grinning grease-paint—is for all the tragedy of the human condition.

"Would you like a drink?" he asks, with simple, unforced generosity. You watch him as he mixes it, and see not the dreamer of the *Horror Crypt* but the practical man who could have carved out a career for himself as a chemist or a soda-jerk. Another side to his character, you realise, and begin to understand that his character is as rich in sides as a threepenny-bit.

And which side, you ask yourself, is the real Tramplin? You search for some sort of clue to his true self. Is there one in the way he dresses, with socks inside his shoes and grey trousers? Is there one in the story of his childhood—brought up by his father and mother and educated at school, an experience which was to leave the multiplication tables and the elements of reading and writing deeply etched upon his memory? Or is it in something that Hal Knocker, an old friend from boyhood days, once said to him? "Vic," he said, "thanks a lot for the meal. I'll be seeing you."

"Well," says Tramplin finally, "I have to go and see a man about a dog." Perhaps this is the real Tramplin, you feel—the shy man who flees human contact and seeks the rich and simple companionship of the animal kingdom. As you leave, you snatch one of Tramplin's buttons as a keepsake. But you take with it something more precious still—the knowledge that the enigma of Victor Tramplin's personality remains as inviolate as when you arrived.

Every Day in Every Way

If there's one thing I enjoy it's curling up with a good book entitled *Release Your Hidden Personality—and Find God!* or *How to Sell Friends and Merchandise People*. At the moment I am curled up with the latest of these treasure chests of wisdom, *Word Power—Life Power*, by one Vernon Howard.

Sooner or later, I am sure, *Reader's Digest* will regurgitate the quintessential cud of Mr. Howard's argument, but for readers who would prefer it in tablet form here and now it is roughly "Say beautiful things, and you will be a beautiful person."

What I enjoy are the anecdotes these books abound in, about

nerve-racked, unsuccessful salesmen who go groaning to their doctor, a chuckling, genial old bird who gives them a simple mnemonic to remember, equipped with which they swiftly become president of the company, turning up under a thin disguise one or two anecdotes later to chuckle genially and show the reporter who is asking them for the secret of their success the letters "C.G." carved on their wall (standing for "Chuckle Genially").

Apart from chuckling, the basic technique for self-improvement is usually a programme of exercises and mnemonics with which the reader is urged to keep pounding away at himself all the time. Mr. Howard, for example, suggests repeating phrases like "My words are daily dynamite," "I rest in the best!" and "A smile is my style!" He would also like you to "create vitalising verbal visions—don't just day-dream," "build your dream castles with constructive word-nails," "try the 'tomato technique,'" "bake a say-cake!" (which consists of a cupful of cheery remarks, a generous amount of enthusiasm, a full quart of prayer, and a pint of humour), and "make every adverb a gladverb."

A devotee of these pep books (particularly if he is trying to put more than one of them into practice at the same time) must maintain inside his head an interior monologue unsurpassed in richness since James Joyce ceased creating his vitalising verbal visions. Take the case of Walter, for instance. Walter, an elastic-hosiery salesman is driving back to his head office in Walsall after being tossed out into the street by a chuckling cheesemonger in Rugeley. He has a hangover, an overdraft, and good reason to believe he is just about to be declared redundant.

"I'm feeling fine," he is saying to himself as he drives along. "Things fine are mine. I rest in the best. I bask in the task. I wash in the slosh. Uh-huh, wrong one there. Try the tomato technique, instead. Just a moment—which is the tomato technique? Forgotten. Oh, well, all I need to do is use the cucumber technique for remembering things. How does that go? H'm, seem to have forgotten that one, too.

"Never mind, keep smiling. A smile is my style. Check smile in driving mirror. Look out! Damn' fool of a woman stepping off the kerb then! They ought to flog jay-walkers!

Calm down. Make every adjective a gladjective. That's wrong. What the hell is it? Every noun a gloun? God, I feel shaky. Nonsense. Never felt better. Things mine are fine. Every verb a glerb.

"Headache. Pain in back. Quick, some constructive word-nails. Create a verbalised, visual vitamin ... a virtualised, verbal victual ... skip it. Try baking a say-cake. A cupful of word-nails, a quart of gladverbs ... gladverbs! That's the word! Slow down for this roundabout, now. Watch for the posting to Gladverb.

"I'm fine. Things fine are mine. I roast on toast. The toast floating down the Rhine, and the Rhine coasting down my spine. Now steady. Get a grip. Try laughing. Can't. Say 'ha.' Now say 'ha' again. Ha-ha. That's laughing. I laugh in the bath. I bath in the laugh.

"Funny. Been going round this roundabout for a long time, but still no posting to Gladsall. Ah, policeman waving on the paving. Stop and ask him. Wind down window. Now, big, big smile, friendly slap on back for copper, never felt better. Officer, there's no posting boasting Gladby. I mean Gladsall. No, no, Gladverb. What? Get out and walk along that white line? Why, certainly. Big smile, feeling fine. Both feet upon the line, like a bug upon a vine, feeling fine, fine, fine...."

Gagg Speaks

"How," I have sometimes heard people gasp admiringly as they looked at the work of this country's cartoonists, "do these chaps manage to make their stuff so true to life? How do they discover the situations which mirror the human predicament and the world as it is today with such accuracy and originality?"

I put these razor-sharp questions to one of our leading cartoonists, Gagg, at his semi-detached residence in the cartoonist belt. "It's easy," he replied. "I simply draw the world around me and life as I see it lived in my own family circle from day to day."

Q.: Perhaps you would describe a typical day, Mr. Gagg.

A.: Certainly. First of all I take a bath, in the middle of which I am always called to the door or the telephone with a towel round my waist. At breakfast, of course, I find myself completely hidden behind the morning paper, a situation which gives my wife (not a comely woman, I am afraid, and a head taller than me) the opportunity for some highly risible remark. Then off to the office. I still sometimes leave without my trousers—very amusing!—though less frequently than in the past. Trousers or no trousers, on the Tube I invariably look over my neighbour's shoulder at his paper.

Q.: And when you get to the office?

A.: The first task is to indulge in some humorous badinage or repartee with The Boss, as he is called, over my lateness. Then my secretary sits down in my lap and we start the day's work.

Q.: Why does your secretary sit in your lap?

A.: It seems to be a tradition of the firm. I believe it dates from the years of austerity, when chairs were difficult to come by, and has been kept on as an uplifting mortification of the flesh for both parties.

Q.: Does she remain there all day?

A.: No. Occasionally I have to go and ask the boss for a rise. He can never afford to give me one, of course: the line on the sales graph slumps so sharply it has to be continued down the wall, and men with masks and horizontally striped vests keep robbing the safe. The police who chase them, incidentally, are for some reason usually American.

Q.: And when you get home at the end of a hard day?

A.: I find that the Little Woman, as she is called, has crashed the car while trying to get it in the garage. I am further enraged to discover that she has bought a new spring hat. Nor is this all. The supper she has cooked turns out to be burnt to a cinder, and when I make some humorous reproach about it she packs a bag and returns to her mother. I try to console myself with a little Indian snake-charming, but it's no use. There is nothing for it but to go out to a public-house and drown my sorrows.

Q.: Are you successful?

A.: Entirely. As the evening wears on my collar becomes

loosened, my hair gets dishevelled, and my shpeech grows shlurred. On my way home I shtop to shupport a shtreet-lamp under a creshent moon and find that I am wearing a battered top-hat and a somewhat disharrayed evening dresh.

Q.: *The scene you have depicted a hundred times.*

A.: Yes, indeed. Like the ensuing scene, when I reach home and find that my wife is waiting for me with a rolling-pin. A poignant moment.

Q.: *And then to sleep?*

A.: Far from it. I lie tossing and turning on my bed of nails for a long time, counting sheep which get up to the most amusing antics inside their balloons. But I have to go down to throw out my daughter's young man, who has still not left, and who is kneeling in front of her with some ludicrous proposal of marriage. Then I am called away to the local maternity hospital, where my wife is now confined. The nurses hold a highly rib-tickling assortment of monkeys and other animals up to the glass of the waiting-room before my quadruplets arrive.

Q.: *Quadruplets, Mr. Gagg?*

A.: I'm afraid so. A truly phenomenal output of children has to be maintained to be eaten by wild animals at the zoo.

Q.: *Do you get any time at all in the comfort of your bed of nails?*

A.: A little. I usually spend it dreaming about a holiday I should like to take one day, shipwrecked on a very small desert island with one palm tree. Oh, it's a full and satisfying life, you know. We don't aspire to the sort of society where you find ladies labelled "Peace," or piebald horses inscribed "Arab resentment over British Middle East policy." But for ordinary folk who like familiar things spiced with a bit of sub-human interest, you can't beat it.

Plain Speaking on S'Agaro

Having just come back from a holiday in Spain I can tell you one thing about that part of the world; they speak a pretty peculiar sort of language down there. I was given a trilingual guide-book to the Costa Brava—or, rather, to what it insisted on calling the "main accidents" of the area—which has tied several reef-knots and a running bowline in my powers of communication. The accident the author cares most about is a town called S'Agaro. Well, it's a non-town. I mean, it's a happy conjuncture. I mean—well, let *him* explain it:

S'AGARO TODAY

S'Agaro is neither a town nor a history: S'Agaro is a happy conjuncture, an inquietude felt since few years—25—and in its boundaries, everything except the Nature is recent. This is why S'Agaro becomes unistakable.

Besides being a personal discovery (it is known to be the work of a sole man) it is a harmony become possible where heretofore was not anything else than savage rocks, rough, full with thick woods and wild vegetation, where the beach of San Pol, belonging to San Feliu de Guixols, ended. Mr. Ensesa felt once the calling of S'Agaro. That landscape, hostile and rejected, was keenly studied with the collaboration of the architect Mr. Santiago Maso Valenti. After four years they gave rise to this light and wonderful reality of the S'Agaro of today, abridgment of beauty, harmony, good taste, and selectness.

The general plann, ruled to the least details, has become his miracle of synchronism in the style and the ambient. The buildings in their totality the same as the wonderful gardens and works to embellish the whole urbinisation have followed the same rule and have not deserted the collective soul. There is not in S'Agaro a single eccentricity for the edge of those architectonic monsters with which another urban-isations are so full. . . . In S'Agaro the tourist finds that "it" he missed. This "it" so social, and elegant, so subtle and poetic. Within its district the whole "grand monde" collects in formal parties, international sport contests, all this gives it the fame that enjoys everywhere in the world.

After this, the author apparently felt too confused and exhausted to go on to "S'Agaro, Tomorrow." But here, for those who care, is a play entitled *S'Agaro, Yesterday*, an unhappy conjuncture of inquietudes I shall be putting on out there before the grand monde next season. All cheques for tickets should be made payable to the English-Speaking Union.

> *(Scene: S'Agaro heretofore. Not anything else is there than savage rocks, rough, full with wild orange peel. On that savage rock sits Mr. Ensesa and Mr. Valenti, neither towns nor histories, but a felicitous condoublement of humane beings.)*

Mr. Ensesa *(jumping upwards)*: I felt the calling of S'Agaro!

Mr. Valenti: Make no attention, Mr. Ensesa. It is probably just an inquietude felt since eating bad paella for lunch.

S'Agaro *(calling)*: Mr. Ensesa!

Mr. Ensesa *(excitedly)*: The calling is now a two-timing re-duplicature!

> *(They keenly study that landscape, hostile and rejected.)*

Mr. Ensesa: I am missing "it," Mr. Valenti. In all that wild waste of broken sun-tan-lotion bottles is not "it."

Mr. Valenti: You mean that "it" so explicative, so deli-quescent, so uneccentric, Mr. Ensesa?

Mr. Ensesa: It is unistakable. We are missing the "big world" (I translate, of course) collecting in formal parties to play clock-golf and international deck-quoits contests. We are missing—how we say it in Spanish—the *"pesetas."*

Mr. Valenti: Permit me to urbanise this unfelicitous inquietude, Mr. Ensesa. I am architect, well known for urbanising without a single eccentricity for the edge of those architectonic monsters with which some urbanisations I could mention are so full.

Mr. Ensesa: If your plans are as harmonious as your words,

Mr. Valenti, S'Agaro will indeed be a dish for the dogs. Can you give rise to abridgments?

Mr. Valenti: Abridgments, atunnelments, ahousements, anything.

Mr. Ensesa: Then give rise to an abridgment of beauty, harmony, good taste, and selectness.

(While Mr. Valenti savagely abridges these, reducing them to mere shadows of their former selves, a kind of prophetic radiance plays about Mr. Ensesa's head.)

Mr. Ensesa *(rhapsodically)*: In years to come, all the peoples will be regarding our happy inquietude and calling it "a miracle of synchronism in the style and the ambient." Or maybe "a stylistic synchro-mesh in ambulating mirror-cells." Or perhaps even "an ambidextrous cyclotron called Mirabelle Stylites."

(He stops to consider the point, but by this time, so thoroughly has Mr. Valenti abridged everything, the curtain has come down and the band is playing "God Save Our Gracious Dictator." Oh, well, I've just realised what the guide-book is getting at when it calls S'Agaro an inquietude and a happy conjuncture—it means it's a noisy but cheerful joint. Let's dance.)

Housebiz

I wonder if a little more interest in politics might be aroused if politicians cast modesty aside and displayed that total self-absorption which film stars always seem to be able to put over so effectively in interviews. Well, here's a trial run I did with Mr. Nigel Sharpe-Groomsman MP, star of Parliament and Tory Party Conference.

Good morning, Mr Sharpe-Groomsman.

Call me Nigel, Mike.

Nigel, you're appearing at the moment in the Infectious Aliens (Exclusion) Bill, aren't you?

That's right, Mike. It's a fearless, controversial bill, of

course, but it's immensely human and worthwhile. My role is to stand up and speak out in favour of the brotherhood of man. Of course everyone thinks I'm letting the side down, but in the end I turn out to be loyal after all when I produce horrifying figures of Danes and Dutchmen arriving with influenza, and I vote with the Government.

It sounds a great debate, Nigel.

Yes, it is. The bill's being introduced by my old friend Chris Smoothe. He's a wonderful, wonderful politician, and it's been great fun working with him on this. But then the whole team is absolutely wonderful, and I think we've produced a wonderful, wonderful bill that everyone's going to enjoy a lot.

Is this the first bill you've done with Christopher Smoothe?

No, we were in the Landlords' Protection Bill together in 1960, with Harry Debenture and Simon Sheermurder, and again this year in the Welfare Services (Curtailment) Bill, which broke all records in gross savings at the Treasury. Landlords' Protection, of course, was my first starring part.

You've certainly shot to the top, Nigel. Nigel, is it true that you were first discovered modelling for men's wear advertisements?

Yes, I got my first break through the photograph that caused all the scandal—the one of me in underwear and suspenders. A Conservative Party agent saw it and snapped me up at once.

Tell me, Nigel...

Call me Nige, Mike.

Nige, you've sometimes been described as the new Harold Macmillan.

Yes, Mike, I have. But I've also been called "the new Duncan Sandys," "the new Ernest Marples," and "the new Lord Salisbury." I don't like these labels. I should like to be thought of just as myself, Nigel Sharpe-Groomsman. I mean, after all, I'm fundamentally a person in my own right. That's what I want to get over.

You don't think there's any truth in the labels, then?

Oh, I wouldn't say that. I think it's true that I have Duncan's nose and Ernest's legs. But people say I smile like Harold Macmillan. I don't think that's entirely true. When I smile—so I'm told by many critics and political commentators—my whole face lights up in a very individual way. And I don't want to get typecast. I don't always want to be the sort of member who appears to let the side down by talking about the brotherhood of man but who always rallies round and votes for the Government in the end. I mean, I want the public to realise—I want Ministers to realise—that I'm a serious politician. It's not that I haven't enjoyed doing this wonderful, wonderful Infectious Aliens (Exclusion) Bill with Chris, but one has one's career to think of.

One last question, Nige....

Call me Ni, Mike.

What sort of bill would you most like to appear in, Ni?

Well, Mike, I'd like to do a bill which offered a role with a greater chance to express the real me. A war bill, for example, with a debate where I call for courage and sacrifice from the nation in face of overwhelming odds. I mean, basically I'm the Churchill type. My friends all tell me I've got Churchill's ears.

Thanks for coming along, Ni. I'm sure we'll all be watching you tomorrow in the Infectious Aliens (Exclusion) Bill.

The Great Shikar of 1896

"Sir," says a letter from one Captain P. Horrocks Boothroyd in the *Field*, "the standards of the shooting field have declined steadily since the First World War. I remember loading for my father, a widely respected shot, both in India and England. The stress he laid on correct dress was proverbial. On one famous occasion Lord M., when still a subaltern, was sent home by my father, his colonel, for turning up at the Rajah's annual tiger hunt with two of the buttons on his spats undone. He was no less severe on himself. He missed what is generally considered to have been the finest *shikar* of 1896 because his best solar topi had been sat upon by my *ayah*, and he refused to shoot with the Governor in his pig-sticking topi.

"It is only just that the fall in sartorial correctitude has been followed by a decline in the bags obtained. The sight of long-haired hobbledehoys, dressed in whipcord slacks, a sort of brown dancing pump, a vividly coloured jersey, and, to crown the whole dreadful *ensemble*, a 'Robin Hood' hat, usually worn on the back of the over-pomaded head, drives me so wild with rage that my shooting suffers."

I feel an instinctive bond with Captain Boothroyd, for by a queer coincidence none of my forebears shot at that *shikar* in 1896 either. None of them would have considered for a moment going near the Governor in a pig-sticking *topi*. They wouldn't have been able to touch their forelocks quickly enough.

But what a *shikar* it was! Back in England, Marie Lloyd was packing them in at the Old Vic with Noël Coward's wonderful "Tea for Two." Everyone was dancing the daring new Black Bottom. Income tax was twopence in the pound, and wonderful, wonderful Queen Victoria looked as if she would live for ever.

At Bangalore, the day of the *shikar* dawned bright and clear. The Indian servants, with simple devotion, had been up all night pipeclaying the *sahibs'* underwear and putting green blanco on the grass. By dawn the landscape was in a very correct state indeed, and Colonel Boothroyd's absence showed up sharply against it. The Governor's irritation, however, quickly subsided when it was explained that owing to the *ayah's* malfeasance with the solar *topi* the Colonel hadn't a thing to wear, *mydeah*. The absence of Ebenezer Frayn, however, caused rather more of a stir.

"Where the devil is that *fellah* Frayn?" demanded the Governor. "What's the good of a *butlah* if he doesn't polish the *aspidistrahs* with the rest of the *laybah* force?"

"I believe some *jokah* has sat on his *bhola*, Your Excellency," replied young Lord Mulligatawny, hastily buttoning up his lavender gloves, "and he's not a man who would care to be seen in a *trilbi*."

"Naturally. But has he no *toppah*?"

"He has, sir, but he refuses to wear it to work without a *clowthin' allowahns*."

"Dammit, Mulligatawny, this is the start of the Indian Mutiny! Turn the guns on him."

"*Rajah*, sir."

A party of *beatahs* quickly drove Frayn towards the guns.

He looked an absolute *boundah* in his pork-butchering *bhota*, and made his appearance worse by carrying a *bannah* saying "No victimisation! Hands off Ebenezer Frayn!"

The *shikar* that followed was voted by Indians present to be the finest not only of 1896, but of 1897 and 1898 as well. The sight of that long-haired hobbledehoy with the over-pomaded hair—my forebear, I'm afraid—drove the impeccably turned out shooting party so wild with rage that their markmanship went gravely astray, and great carnage broke out, beginning with the death of Colonel Trumbellow of the Third Foot (he had lost the first two at Lucknow).

"The Gatling's *jahmd*," Lord Mulligatawny was soon reporting to the Governor, flicking a little powder blackening off his spats, "and the Colonel's *dehd*, and the sands of the desert are sodden *rehd*."

"Do up your bottom waistcoat button," replied the Governor coldly. "We'd have the *trousahs* off the *blightah*, but it's only to be expected that your sartorial incorrectitude should be followed by a decline in the bags obtained."

Oh, it was quite a *shikar*. It may be coincidence, but there's a little yellow idol to the north of Katmandu inscribed: "To the *ayah* who sat on my solar *topi*. In eternal gratitude. Colonel B."

Never Put Off to Gomorrah

... the proposals in your Note can only meet with unqualified rejection, while the proposals I have set forth above, on the other hand, contain the basis of equitable negotiation in the cause of world virtue, leading eventually to the total liquidation of unrighteousness which is undoubtedly the dearest and most heartfelt wish of the peoples of our two great cities.

N. S. LESS, *Lord Mayor of Sodom*

My dear Lord Mayor,

I have now been able to study very carefully your reply of

February 22 to my Note of February 12 to my reply of February 10, for which I thank you. I see with regret that its main proposal is the one which you put forward in your earlier Notes, of October 14, November 1, December 9, January 12, January 20, etc., calling for any conference on reducing the level of unrighteousness to be preceded by a meeting of the civic heads of our two cities.

This, as I explained in my Notes of October 17, November 3, December 12, January 15, January 28, and February 12, is unacceptable. I do not believe, as I said in those Notes, that any useful purpose would be served by an unprepared meeting of civic heads at this stage. What we have to do before we meet, I am convinced, is to create confidence by achieving some actual progress in reducing the dangerously high level of unrighteousness in our two cities before—as so many experts have warned us is possible—it leads to a disastrous holocaust in which both our cities would be destroyed.

On the necessity of reducing unrighteousness all thinking men are, I am sure, agreed. What is at issue between us is the extremely complex technical question of how such a reduction can best be achieved. I note with regret your rejection of my proposal (put forward in my Notes of October 17, November 3, December 12, January 15, January 28, and February 12) for a stage-by-stage reduction under adequate safeguards and controls.

Let me say once again that I believe—and my Corporation believes—that before there can be any agreement to reduce unrighteousness, provision must be made for adequate inter-city inspection to ensure that the agreed level is not exceeded. Here I must reject as entirely false your allegation, set forth in your Notes of October 14, etc., and previously rebutted in my Notes of October 17, etc., that my intention in putting forward this plan is to establish, under a cloak of respectability, an espionage service for discovering details of your secret and advanced vices which would be commercially useful to us. Such a suggestion can only be intended to serve the purposes of propaganda. The real reason, as I have explained in earlier notes, is to obviate the danger—presented by your proposal for unverified reduction—that one of the parties, while storing up credit in Heaven by publicly liquidating the forces of vice, might in secret be building up other vices, so obtaining an unfair advantage in the tourist trade.

I do not wish at this stage to go into this too deeply. My point is that here is a clearly defined area of disagreement between us of the sort which would have to be explored by specialists in moral hygiene with positive results before any general question of morals could be usefully discussed at the summit. It was with the aim of obtaining expert exploration of these areas that I proposed a disunrighteousness conference to take place first (my Notes of October 14, etc.). I suggest, as a measure of compromise, that this conference should be preceded by a meeting of town clerks to prepare an agenda for the conference, though with the limitation, naturally, that this agenda should exclude any consideration of an unverified reduction.

It is in no spirit of mere propaganda, but in the hope that you will respond to the desperate yearnings of the common people in both our cities for righteousness that I urge you to consider this proposal.

J. F. MORE, Lord Mayor of Gomorrah

My dear Lord Mayor,

I must say frankly that I am deeply grieved by the negative attitude adopted in your reply of February 25 to my note of February 22 to your reply of February 12 to my note of February 10 to your . . .

Listener Sport

Why people watch sport baffles me. But why they listen in their millions to a wireless commentator watching it on their behalf numbs even my faculty of bafflement. I wonder if it's just sport they are eager to experience vicariously, or whether they would find a new pleasure in, say, discussion programmes presented this way?

*   *   *

. . . And here in the studio in Maida Vale we're just waiting for the team to emerge from the Hospitality Room for the 143rd session of Top Topic. It was rather cold in the studio earlier on, but it's warming up now, and the patches of damp you could see around the walls in the early afternoon have almost dried out.

And now here comes the team, led by their chairman, O. J. Sprout, the well-known literary critic and man of letters, followed by Sir Harold Sidewinder, the grand old man of so many walks of life, Lady Frigate, woman of opinion, and Ken Nocker, the teenage satirist.

Now, while they take their places round the table, let's look at the form. Sir Harold Sidewinder, of course, has appeared in this programme 18 times before, though only twice in this studio, and on those two occasions he seemed slightly worried by the tricky north-east draught for which this studio is notorious. . . . And now I think O. J. Sprout is about to deliver the first topic. No, there's still some delay about positioning the team. As I was saying, Sir Harold's analysis over the 18 programmes was 147,000 words for 31 topics raised, which . . .

Oh, the first topic's away, and it's a beauty! Sprout raised it very easily and naturally, almost as if he was lobbing a topic of conversation on to his own breakfast-table. And he's nodded to Lady Frigate. Lady Frigate moves in smoothly to pick it up—you can see from her technique that she is an old What's My Salary? player. On the top of her form this season, too.

With a quick flutter of the eyelashes she rephrases the topic so that—yes—so that its meaning is reversed, and swiftly dismisses it. Away goes the first topic of the programme, with all the sting taken out of it, into Sir Harold Sidewinder's lap.

Sir Harold swings at it easily, as if he had all the time in the world. What a grand old exponent of the game he is! There are few men half his age who could put yet another twist on an already twisted meaning with that aplomb. What's he up to? Is he . . . ? Yes, he is—he's explaining very steadily and easily that the topic as he has now formulated it reminds him of something Lord Curzon told him in 1910.

Now while Sir Harold is telling his story—with the score standing at one down and one to play on the first topic of the 143rd session of Top Topic—I'll just say a word about Ken

Nocker, whose first appearance in Top Topic this is. He's a forceful young player who has attracted a great deal of attention by his immensely aggressive, hard-hitting approach. It's the sort of play that the crowd finds very attractive, and ...

Hello, what's this? Ken has cut in on Sir Harold's graceful stone-walling with a very sharp tackle. Sprout intervenes. But now it's Nocker again, going like the wind. Nocker to Sidewinder. Sidewinder to Nocker. Sprout tries to tackle Nocker, but Frigate cuts in.... And it's Frigate to Nocker, Nocker to Sidewinder, Sidewinder to Sprout, Nocker again, still Nocker....

Now there's a general free-for-all, with the topic in the middle somewhere, I think, and everyone going like mad. I can't quite see ... I think it's Frigate ... no, it's Sidewinder ... no, I'm wrong, it's Nocker, and this is sensational, it's unbelievable.... Sidewinder's leaning back looking very tired—I don't think he can last much longer—and it's Nocker, Nocker all the way. No! Yes! No! Yes, it is. It's Nocker's point, and the applause-meter shows that at the end of the first topic in the 143rd Top Topic the score is 1–0, with the topic "Is the crime wave due to all this psychology we hear so much about?" voted as likely to get into this week's top twenty topics in the news.

And now, while we're waiting for the next topic to be raised, I'll just give you a words-per-topic analysis of the last 50 programmes....

Chez Crumble

One of the principal benefits that matrimony confers on the young professional class is that it enables us to give up that tiresome pretence of being interested in spiritual and cultural matters—forced on us by our education and our courtship rituals—and lets us settle down to a frank and total absorption in our financial and material circumstances.

When, for instance, you call on the newly married Crumbles—formerly socially conscious Christopher Crumble and sensitive, musical Lavinia Knudge—do you talk about the problems of secondary education, or English choral music of the sixteenth century, as you would have done back in the good old days of Crumble and Knudge? You do not. Because Lavinia says...

Lavinia: Before you do anything else, you must come and look over the flat!

Christopher: ... that's right, just take your coat off—I'll hang it on this automatic coat-rack. ...

Lavinia: ... which Christopher made himself, didn't you, darling?

Christopher: Got a kit from Rackkitz of Wembley—costs about half the price of an ordinary automatic coat-rack...

Lavinia: ... and it's fire-resistant, too...

Christopher: ... now this is the hall, of course...

Lavinia: ... which we made ourselves by partitioning off part of the bedroom...

Christopher: ... with half-inch Doncaster boarding, at a shilling a foot, if you know the right place...

Lavinia: ... Christopher got it from the brother of an old school-friend of his, didn't you, darling? Now—mind your head on that steel brace—this is the bedroom...

Christopher: ... we picked up the bed for a song in a little shop I know in Edmonton...

Lavinia: ... and fitted it out with a Dormofoam mattress. They're so much the best, of course. In fact there's a waiting-list for Dormofoams, but we had tremendous luck and got one ordered for someone who died...

Christopher: ... and this is the kitchen opening off in the corner here. It was really the handiness of having the kitchen opening directly into the bedroom that made us take the flat...

Lavinia: ... you should have seen it when we first moved in! But Christopher had the brilliant idea of covering up the holes in the floor with some special asbestos his uncle makes ...

Christopher: ... so we got a discount on it. We're frightfully proud of that stainless steel bootrack, by the way. I don't know whether you saw it recommended in *Which?* last month...?

Lavinia: ... it's so much more practical than all those

silver-plated ones you see in the shops. According to *Which*? they pounded it with 140 average boot-impacts an hour for 17 days before it collapsed...

Christopher: ... I'd take you out to show you the lavatory, but it is raining rather hard. Remind us you haven't seen it next time you come, won't you, and we'll make a point of it...

Lavinia: ... and here we are in the living-room...

Christopher: ... have you seen this Plushco plastic carpeting before? We think it's awfully good, don't we, darling? Half the price of ordinary carpet, and terrifically hard-wearing. We've had it down, what, two weeks now? Not a sign of wear on it...

Lavinia: ... I see you're looking at all those old books on music and education. You won't believe it, but we had those shelves built for five pounds—timber and all...

Christopher: ... by a marvellous little man we found by sheerest chance in Muswell Hill. Remind me to give you his address...

Lavinia: ... though I think he did it specially cheaply for us just because he happened to take to us...

Christopher: ... by the way, would you like a glass of Sardinian sherry?

Lavinia: ... we've developed rather a thing about Sardinian sherry, haven't we, darling?

Christopher: ... we get it by the gallon from a little shop in Sydenham. Found the place by sheer chance...

Lavinia: ... tremendously practical, and it works out at six-and-four a bottle...

Christopher: ... incidentally, what do you think we pay for the flat? No, go on, have a guess ... Well, I'll tell you—five pounds a week...

Lavinia: ... it's an absolute bargain, of course. We only found it through a friend of my mother's, who just by sheerest chance happened to be...

Christopher: ... I say, you're looking rather groggy. Lavinia, darling, run and fetch him some Asprilux. I don't know whether you've tried Asprilux, but we think it's much better than any of the other brands of aspirin ... No, sit in this chair—it's got a rather ingenious reclining back—we just got the last one to be made. Comfortable, isn't it? What do you think of Lavinia, by the way? Such practical, easy-to-clean hands and feet. You won't believe it, but I picked her up by the sheerest chance at a little bookshop I know down in Wimbledon...

Bodbury: The Nation Waits

Any moment now (*said Brian Bright, the well-known television personality*), any moment now the candidates and the returning officer will be appearing on that small balcony there on the front of the Town Hall, and we shall hear the result, we shall hear the result of the Bodbury byelection. There's been a series of delays—the announcement was expected much earlier than this—but I think, we think, we've had word that the result of the Bodbury byelection, the result, here, in Bodbury, of the byelection, the Bodbury byelection, should be coming through very shortly.

When it does, the returning officer will come through that door, at the back of the balcony. With him will be the three candidates. All three of them, with the returning officer, will come on to the balcony, through the door at the back. And it'll be on that balcony, the one you can see there, on the front of the Town Hall, that he, that the returning officer, will announce the result, the result of the Bodbury byelection.

I think there must be another delay. There's no sign of them. We heard, we learnt a few minutes ago that the returning officer would be coming out very shortly, but there's still no sign of him, so I think we must conclude—because we did hear he was on his way and he hasn't come—I think we must conclude that there's some delay.

I'll take the opportunity to remind you that we're in front of the Town Hall at Bodbury, waiting for the result of the byelection, the Bodbury byelection. There's great speculation here about the result among the very large and cheerful crowd in the square—or there was, until they all went home to bed. It could be a Conservative victory, if the Liberal and Labour candidates

41

haven't done as well as they might. It could be a win for Labour, with the Conservatives at the bottom of the poll— depending on how well the Liberals have done. Or, of course, the Liberal swing could have put the Liberal in, if it was strong enough, if it was strong enough to put the Liberal in.

Well, here we are, then, still waiting for the result, for the result of the Bodbury byelection. If the swing to Labour is more marked than the trend to Liberal, or vice versa, then there's a chance, I think there's a fair chance, that he, whichever one it is, may profit from it—that's to say, from the swing. Or the trend, of course. If not, then, of course, not. And if the inevitable mid-term dissatisfaction with the Government means, as it may, that the Conservative gets *fewer* votes than the other candidates, then I think there's a pretty strong possibility he won't get in.

We spoke to a Conservative voter earlier in the evening, here in the main square, and asked him which way he had voted, and he said Conservative. I think that may be a pointer, it may be some sort of indication. I think it may go to show that if the trend shown at Bodbury is followed throughout the rest of the country, then the result here may may be a guide to the way the trend is going. But if the result here is not going to be repeated in other constituencies, then it's no use, no use at all, taking it as any sort of guide.

We shall know, of course, when the results are brought out, in the traditional way, through that door at the back of the balcony, by the returning officer, who will open the door at the back of the balcony, and come out with the candidates, through the door, to read the results, from the balcony.

Still no sign. If the absence of swing, either to the left or to the right, shown by the door at the back of the balcony, is any pointer at all, it points, it points to a natural mid-term dissatis- faction among returning officers with bringing the result through the door at the back of the balcony, and indicates a growing trend, a fast-growing trend, to the sort of situation where all three of the candidates are left to swing from the front of the balcony, there, on the Town Hall, and we can all go home and have breakfast, have breakfast in a beautiful totalitarian silence...

Bodbury Speaks Out!

F. Muncher (Lab.)   14,931
J. P. R. Cramshaw-Bollington (C)   8,101
S. W. Dearfellow (L)   7,123

Labour majority 6,830

(*General election:* Lab. 23,987; C 16,021; L 9,980. Lab. maj.—7,966)

F. Muncher: It's a wonderful result. Not only have we held the seat, but we have increased our share of the poll—a real smack in the eye for the Government. The voters of Bodbury have told Mr Macmillan and his friends in no uncertain terms what they think of the Government's record on such things as the Common Market (or will have done, as soon as we have actually decided which policy on this question it was that our supporters were voting for). And if you take our vote in conjunction with the Liberal vote, it's clear that there is an overwhelming anti-Tory majority in Bodbury.

J. P. R. Cramshaw-Bollington: I'm absolutely delighted with the result. At a time when the pendulum traditionally swings against the party in office, we've slashed the Labour majority in this Labour stronghold. I take this as a most encouraging vote of confidence in the Government—a message from the people of Bodbury to Mr Macmillan, urging him to carry on with the good work, whatever it may be. And taking the increased Liberal vote into account, its evident that there is a definite anti-Socialist majority in Bodbury.

S. W. Dearfellow: The result couldn't be better. Our share of the vote is up sharply, while the numbers of votes polled by both the Labour and Conservative candidates have slumped heavily. This is Bodbury's way of saying "A plague on both your houses—we want to have it both ways with the

Liberals." And if you take the Liberal vote in conjunction with either the Labour or the Conservative vote, you can see that either way we've got a clear anti-extremist majority.

Sprout: Thank you, gentlemen. Now, what do the commentators think about the national significance of the Bodbury result? Haddock?

Haddock: Well, it should give real encouragement to the Liberals. But then again, it might be said that though they have gained, they have gained much less than might have been expected. And since anyway the gain will almost certainly disappear again at a general election, I feel they should temper their encouragement with a feeling of disappointment.

Trouncer: I interpret the quite noticeable fall in the Labour majority as a clear endorsement of the Government's position on manganese quotas. However, this fall was accompanied by an increase in Labour's share of the vote, which suggests to me a movement of Conservative supporters who have become disillusioned by the Government's record on departmental procedure reform.

Pinn: Though since the actual *size* of the Labour vote fell, this movement may have been accompanied by the abstention of Labour voters disillusioned with the Opposition's record on the same question. Or perhaps with Harold Wilson's personality. Or George Brown's face.

Sprout: To me, I must say, the real meaning of Bodbury lies in the reduction of the Conservative vote, which spells out in words of one syllable comprehensible to even the dullest back-bencher that there is no support in the country for the Government's lukewarm attitude to Chile.

Haddock: Possibly. The permutations are endless. And when one considers the local factors...

Trouncer: ... the possibility that Fred Muncher's local reputation as deputy chairman of the Bodbury Amateur Weight-Lifters' Association was cancelled out by xenophobic suspicion of his living a quarter of a mile outside the constituency boundary...

Pinn: ... and whether the Liberal gain from middle-class resentment against credit restrictions stopping the building of a new cricket pavilion was balanced by the propaganda effect of

44

the Cramshaw-Bollington Dogs' Home founded by the Conservative candidate's father...

Haddock: ... and whether the rain in the morning hindered the Tories more than the fog in the evening deterred the Socialists...

Sprout: ... one realises that there is plenty of scope yet for imaginative conjecture about what the voters thought they were voting for, provided no unspeakable blackleg actually goes and finds out by asking them.

The Sunshine Life

"If you had more leisure time for 'Sunshine Living,'" says the cereal packet which leers at me across the orange-juice every morning, distracting me from my devotional contemplation of the day's disarmament proposals, "tell us how you would spend it (not more than 15 words)."

Quite a challenge. La Rochefoucauld himself, I should think, would have been pushed to get his thoughts on the subject into fifteen words. But when the manufacturers have empanelled, to judge the aphorisms submitted, the Cookery Editor of *Woman's Own*, Miss Barbara Towle of the Lux Washability Bureau, and Miss Kathleen Harrison, well-known stage, radio, and TV actress, an aspiring young literary man like myself has to take it seriously. My entry is still a shade over fifteen words, but there's precious little sunshine left in it as it stands, and if I cut it any more it may give the effect of a total eclipse.

8.0 a.m.: Wake up. Lie in bed planning best use of day's sunshine leisure to accommodate looking at uplifting newspapers, reading uplifting book, going to uplifting play.

8.30: Fall asleep again.

10.0: Wake up with guilty start. Rush unshaven into breakfast.

10.5: Make up for lost time by simultaneously eating breakfast and working guilt about late rising off on wife—snarling

45

"Why coffee now cold?" "Why fatuous competition on side cereal packet?" etc.

10.45: Reconsider planning of now slightly reduced supply of sunshine leisure.

11.0: Start on uplifting papers. Read uplifting book reviews, film reviews, theatre reviews, opera reviews, radio reviews, television reviews, record reviews.

12.0: Take short rest, snarling about superabundance of reviews in world.

12.10: Remember have not read uplifting ballet reviews. Read them, snarling.

12.30: Decide too little time left before lunch to be worth starting uplifting book. Instead daydream of having unlimited leisure for sunshine living filled with reading uplifting books, seeing uplifting plays, etc.

1.0: Wife summons to lunch. Remember have not yet shaved. Shave hastily, treat wounds, rush in to lunch. Work off guilt about lateness by snarling at wife "Why soup cold?" "Why you not making cheerful conversation?" etc.

2.0: Realise have whole afternoon of leisure stretching ahead, so no need to rush to uplifting book. Let mind wander on sheer amount of leisure available.

2.30: Remember have not read reviews in uplifting weeklies. Feel moral obligation to get through them before turning to uplifting book.

3.30: Remember have not read reviews in uplifting monthlies. Read them, driven on by terrible fear of losing touch with world of uplift.

5.0: Hurl self at last on uplifting book, but before have digested first paragraph of distinguished literary man's critical introduction, wife brings tea.

5.30: Wipe jam off critical introduction. Remember have not studied uplifting consumer research magazine's critical review of jams. Do so. Discover have smeared critical introduction with bad buy.

7.25: Snatch up uplifting book once more. Race through whole page. Wife shouts presence required at dinner. Discover have been reading editor's list of acknowledgements.

7.30: In to dinner with rush to avoid further guilt feelings. Snarl at wife "Why soup now so hot?" "Why so full of bright conversation when husband suffering severe oral scalding?"

8.15: Decide will go with wife to see uplifting play. Forgotten which most uplifting. Reread theatre reviews in uplifting dailies, weeklies, monthlies.

8.40: Realise now too late to get to play. Uplifting film? Reread uplifting film reviews at great speed. Hurl on overcoats. Rush wildly in direction cinema.

9.40: Arrive cinema. Find uplifting film shown first, now over. Realise if rush home will just be in time to watch uplifting television programme reviewing daily newspapers.

11.30: Bed. Fall into exhausted half-sleep, racked by anxiety dream in which have guilty feeling am missing uplifting Sunday papers—containing reviews of uplifting television programme which was reviewing uplifting papers reviewing uplifting television programme reviewing....

D. Op.

Some previously indeterminate figure on the fringes of the middle-men's society, I see, was recently described as "a man of opinion." Now there's a great new rank to aspire to—a high new destiny for all those arts graduates without vocational training who would in the past have ended up as mere "men of letters."

I think I might start studying for it. I should soon be indispensable. Theatre managers would cry "Is there a man of opinion in the house?" and I should stroll nonchalantly up to the stage, only too accustomed to have my evenings off sacrificed to the desperate public need for my professional services.

"Thank God you're here," the theatre manager would say, leading me backstage. "We're in a spot, I can tell you. The stagehands have come out on strike, the juvenile lead's run off with the backer's wife, the backer's withdrawn his money, the Lord Chamberlain's banned the whole of Act Two, and the theatre's on fire."

"It certainly sounds as though you need some frank and stimulating opinions expressed pretty urgently," I should say, settling comfortably into a convenient armchair and sucking on a property pipe. "Let's take the question of striking for a start. It perpetually amazes me that responsible trade union leaders apparently cannot understand that full co-operation with the Government's economic policy is absolutely essential if this country is to be able to afford to keep men of opinion like myself in the style to which we are accustomed. Not that I don't blame the managements as well. In fact I always make a point of blaming both sides in any dispute.

"And that reminds me, in the queer way that we men of opinion are reminded, of another thorny subject—censorship. Now this is a question I have pretty controversial views on. I believe—quite passionately—that we ought to ask ourselves—all of us, you, me, the chap next door—to what extent plays, for example, should be subject to censorship. I know— in my heart—that there are a great many things to be said both for and against it. I'm not going to make any bones about saying frankly that I feel very careful consideration should be given to both sides of the question before we jump to any hasty conclusions.

"You may think that's pretty outspoken. But we have to realise what sort of world we live in—and it's a world where nowadays a juvenile lead doesn't think twice about running off with the backer's wife. I don't know what other people think about this sort of thing, but I can tell you this—whatever they think, I think the opposite. I mean, I could scarcely expect to be paid for my opinions if they were the same as everybody else's, could I?"

By the time I got on to the question of theatrical finance and the human problems behind the enforcement of fire regulations, the crisis would be practically solved, for everyone— delinquent juvenile lead, the enraged backer, his errant wife, and the Lord Chamberlain's stool-pigeons—would all be standing round bewitched by the Orphean flow of melodious opinion.

"What do you think of William Gerhardi as a novelist?" they would demand dreamily. "Do you believe in telepathy?" "Do you agree with Macleod's assessment of Chamberlain?"

48

"Is the dodecaphonic scale an argument for duodecimal arithmetic?"

"Well," I should reply comfortably, "I think a reappraisal of Chamberlain was long overdue. And I'm sure there is some sort of affinity between music and mathematics, though whether the duodecimal system would prove to be more popular than . . . Is the universe expanding? I'm inclined to support the school of thought that holds. . . . What is truth . . .? Wasn't it jesting Pilate who was asked this one, and who . . .? Do I prefer belt or braces? Well, I think the sensible man . . . By the way, is it getting suffocatingly hot in here, or do I really think that by appeasing Chamberlain the duodecimal system could be averted, while the braces are so immensely readable that I incline to the old-fashioned biblical view of the Common Market as being unfair to the older woman, with a crime rate expanding all the time through the baroque splendour of the Soviet leadership into a universe which is, in my view at any rate, just one huge, spongy, gaseous, ectoplasmic mass of stewed opinion . . .?"

A letter from the PUBLISHER

Michael Frankenstein

Every week in this column we tell you the wonderful story of how one section of SPACE MAGAZINE was born. Today we are telling a nativity story so holy, so pregnant with awe, that no man has dared to tell it before—the story of the birth of this column, the Publisher's Letter, itself.

Here at SPACE-DEATH INTERNATIONAL we venerate the Publetter as the inmost shrine of SPACE journalism, the revealed word of the SPACE world-mind. No ordinary column this, but a steely skein of newsprose which is the result of a vast co-ordinated effort by all the manpower at our command. To make the column you are now reading, 1,200 SPACE staffers around the globe filed a word each—and each word was one they had already digested from all the millions of words which were used during the week in the capitals they cover.

An operation like this entails risks, dangers. On his way to file the word "which," *Miguel Freños*, 42, covering the Corunna, Spain, beat, fell into a hole in the road ordered by Corunna's genial public works boss Juan Pepito, 54, and broke his rugged, much-tanned neck.

It also entails long-range planning. Off to Kano, Nigeria, flew Communications Editor *Milo Frangle* to organise the complex task of getting word from remote up-country stringer *Nmikl Mfrayn*. Beaten out over the first stage on jungle drums, the message was taken by camel caravan to Kallamiti, then by age-old traditional post-chaise drawn by highly prized, aphrodisiac-horned rhinoceroses to Katastrofee. Here a specially chartered jet air-liner waited at runway's end with engines blasting. But fog kiboshed a take-off, and at the last moment the whole mammoth organisation was alerted to switch to Plan Two—a picture postcard, on the flip side of which resourceful family man Mfrayn had written the sought-for word—"and."

Back at SPACE-DEATH headquarters, Non-Executive Editor *Martin Faine* spread the collected words over a football-pitch-sized floor area, while Advisory Editor *Max Phrane* indexed and cross-indexed them. But Editorial Editor *Magnus Frenner* was still not satisfied. After an all-night conference with the heads of editorial departments, he ordered a search of the dictionaries. Snapped thrice-fired Frenner, 35: "We've got good words, but there may be better."

Seventy researchers flipped 15,000 pages of ten dictionaries in 25 hours. So heavy was the yield of words from this operation that snowploughs had to be called in to bulldoze a way out of ten-foot word-drifts for word-weary staffers. Only then could Co-ordinating Editor *Morag Sprain* and his team begin the awesome task of sifting out the 700 most telling terms—the weekly winnowing known to hardened SPACE word-birds as "the Big Weed."

Over in the laboratories Analytical Editor *Micah F. Ryan* submitted each of the elite 700 to elaborate tests of spelling and syntax, while behind the scenes SPACE's own corps of under-cover men checked the background of even the humblest preposition for Red influence. Woman's Editor *Mabel Brain*—wife of Pulitzer Prizewinning Dogs Editor *Mumbo Brain*—was summoned from her bed by special messenger at 2 a.m. to come and add the woman's angle, followed shortly by Manipulating Editor *Morry Fryable*, who gave the words the usual slant.

At 6 a.m. world-famous writer *Misha Fraenev* was rushed to the office with siren-wailing squad-car escort to advise on arrangement of the words. Said Fraenev—now through his sixth word-order assignment: "Ask some folk 'How so successful?' Reply I—'Write I like I speak in backward-running, adjective-rich mother tongue Russian.'"

Four Punctuating Editors went without breakfast to get this edition of SPACE out on the streets in time for our mammoth staff of Junior Sales Editors to begin their weekly stint—trying to find anyone not on SPACE staff left in the world to be enrolled as Paying Reading Editors. Even so they'd never have done it, if some compositor hadn't had the sense to dash this alternative piece off and set it up the night before.

Lloyd

A HISTORICAL TRAGI-BUDGET, OR BUDGI-TRAGEDY,
IN FIVE ACTS

(commissioned for the Hoylake Festival, 1994)

Act Three, Scene Four—a Chamber in the Treasury

(*Sennets and tuckets. Enter the Chancellor of the Exchequer, the Lord Privy Purposes, and the Lord Footstool, followed by Under-Secretaries, Parliamentary Private Secretaries, Joint Permanent Secretaries, Under-Secretaries' Private Secretaries, Joint Permanent Secretaries' Under-Secretaries, Fools, and Knaves.*)

Chancellor:
> I saw it in his eyes: he turn'd his gaze
> Upon me, wondrous soft, avuncular,
> Beseech'd me with those pouchèd eyes of his
> As might a man urge on his faithful hound
> To some high eager feat of houndly valour,
> Yea, with an uncle's smile he bade me forth
> To save beloved England's tottering cause
> With one bold coup-de-main of fiscal arms!

Under-Secretaries, etc.:
> Hurrah!
> (*Trumpets, cannons, etc.*)

Lord Footstool:
> 'Tis well said, Chancellor, for Fortune frowns:
> And faceless men do undermine the boroughs,
> Unsettling vacant loons we once call'd ours.

Lord Privy Purposes:
> You mean to take a budget to our woes—
> To beat from metal tempered by the times
> And edg'd upon Necessity's hard stone
> A budget e'en to budget them to death?

Chancellor:
> I do. And with such high intent this day
> Are we three met to forge the cutting steel.

Lord Privy Purposes:
> Acquaint us with your stratagems.

Chancellor:
>   Then hark:
> First will I ease the groaning discontent
> Which freights unjustly those our countrymen
> Whose lawful aspirations soar no higher
> Than purchasing a humble toasting-fork.
> Eleven per cent off toasting-forks, I say!

Lord Footstool:
> This is a wise and bounteous act: the poor
> Will count your name as blessed this day
>   forth.

Chancellor:
> Then will I buy the love of every man
> Who holds the common mousetrap dear: the tax

On mousetraps swoops from nine to eight per
    cent!
Lord Footstool:
    O admirable Chancellor!
Chancellor:
                    But now,
Our forces swoln by loyal mousetrap-men,
And grateful liegemen of the toasting-fork,
We fall like falcons on those jack-a-dandies
Whose foul-brained appetite doth feed on hats,
And scourge them with an added four per cent.
Lord Privy Purposes:
    'Tis well. A hatted man is gallows-bait.
Chancellor:
    And yet my devious stratagem goes further—
Makes pepper-mills more dear, salt-cellars cheap,
Brings Jew's harps down, sends plated shoetrees
    up,
Puts two per cent on fire-dogs, cheapens pins,
Tacks tax on tacks, attacks the tax on ticking.
Lord Privy Purposes:
    Hurt barrel-organs, Chancellor, I pray—
Their monkeys satirise us publicly.
Chancellor:
    Why, so I will. Yet list, we do proceed,
These hair's-weight-balanced dispositions made,
These plots complotted, nimble gin-traps sprung,
At last to strike the boldest blow of all!
And gentlemen not in the Treasury
Will count themselves accurst they were not here
To ride forth on St Crispin Crispian
And cry: Fifteen per cent on lollipops!
Under-Secretaries, etc.:
    Hurrah!
(*Trumpets, cannonades. The Chancellor of the Exchequer
draws his red dispatch-box from its scabbard, and holding it
aloft gallops off in the direction of Agincourt.*)
Lord Privy Purposes:
    Such hair-springs drive the clock of destiny:
Small wonder it still stands at ten to three.

From the Improved Version

The news that the statue of Nkrumah in Accra, which was damaged by an explosion, bore on its side the inscription, "Seek ye first the political kingdom and all the rest shall be added unto you," has touched off a great deal of speculation. Where does the quotation come from? I have heard both the Book of Amazing Free Offers and the Second Book of Unsolicited Testimonials suggested—even the Book of Fub.

In fact, it comes from the Book of Usually Reliable Sources, and was reprinted in that very handy little devotional work for these troubled times, "Selected Wisdom from the Improved Version." In case you are unacquainted with the range and usefulness of this book, or are looking for an inscription of your own, here are a few more extracts:—

Out of the mouths of babes shall come statements of opinion; out of the mouths of princes and counsellors, maid-servants and players of the lute and tabor; and each shall be harkened unto according to his purchasing power. (*Majorities xii 15.*)

The wise king holdeth his tongue before his people, and maketh his servant to speak on his behalf unto the multitude. For if the multitude find fault with his servant's words, then shall the king make public sacrifice of him. And the king shall gain great credit thereby. (*Parliamentarians vii 6.*)

And there was heard the voice of one crying in the metropolis: Come ye to have a drink and meet Rock Richmond, who maketh glad the people with his lute. And this same prophet had a coat of camel's hair, and his meat was oysters and champagne. For he that goeth before must be as empty as the oyster-shell, and his tongue must be soft with wine, that he may become a vessel of smooth and vacant speech. (*Fub. ii 18.*)

If a prince seeketh to increase his army, he summoneth not the servant from his master nor the husband from his wife, lest he maketh them wroth. Rather shall he grind the faces of those warriors he hath imprest before, causing them to toil by night even as by day. For these are already wroth, and their labours will not increase the number of the wrathful, nor doth the law permit them to make known their burden in epistles to the press. (*Majorities v 20.*)

Seek not to share misfortune evenly among the people; but let it bear heavily upon the few. For howsoever sore afflicted they may be, if they cry out thou mayst rebuke them, saying: Ten thousand thousand are them that praise me; what are ye few against this mighty host? The voice that crieth out in you is the voice of devils, yea, and chastisement shall be added to your afflictions. (*Majorities v 23.*)

And he that had mocked the king was brought before him. And the king saith: Mock me again, that I may enjoy that which even the humblest of my subjects hath enjoyed. And the man did as he was bid, and mocked the king, and they that stood about him were sore afraid. But the king betook himself to laughter, and they that were about him did likewise. Then saith the king: Thou shalt have riches, and stay with me, and mock me all the days of my life, that I and no other may have the enjoyment of it. And I shall taste the sweets both of power and of the mockery of power. But when he heard these words, the man was troubled in his soul, and went aside and hanged himself. (*Jokers xiv 2.*)

What shall it avail a man, if he keepeth his own soul but loseth his ministry? (*Parliamentarians ix 3.*)

Sweet is music, and sweet the playing thereof, yet not so sweet as to be honoured in its playing. To be virtuous is worth more than gold; but to be known is more precious than rubies. For all the goings in and the goings out of such a man shall be reported. And his wife shall partake of his glory; yea, and his concubine and his dog. And their opinions shall be sought and prized above the judgments of Solomon. (*Celebrities iii 9.*)

He that findeth old words for new teachings: he is the friend of merchants and the comforter of princes. (*Adverbs i 1.*)

I said, "My Name is 'Ozzy' Manders, Dean of King's"

I must not tell lies.
I must not tell pointless lies.
I must not tell pointless lies at parties.
I must not tell pointless lies at parties when they are plainly going to be found out in the next 10 minutes.
I must not:

1. Let it be thought that I have caught the name of anyone I am ever introduced to, because statistics show that I have never caught anyone's name until I have heard it at least 12 times.

2. Give it to be understood that I have already heard of the owner of the inaudible name, because tests show that apart from one or two obvious exceptions like William Shakespeare and Sir Harold Sidewinder I haven't heard of anyone.

3. Say I have read the man's books, or admired his architecture, or used his firm's brake-linings, or seen his agency's advertisements, or always been interested in his field of research, or know his home town, because I do hereby make a solemn and unconditional declaration, being before witnesses and in sober realisation of my past wrongdoing, that I have done none of these things.

4. Say that I know any of the people he is sure I must know, or have heard of any of the names he takes to be common knowledge, because I don't and haven't, or if I do and have, I've got them all hopelessly mixed up, and when he says Appel I'm thinking of Riopelle, and when he says Buffet I'm thinking of Dubuffet, and when he says Palma I'm thinking of Palermo, and when he says syncretism I'm thinking of syndicalism, and when he says a man called "Pop" Tuddenham who hired a barrage balloon and dressed it up to look like an elephant I'm thinking of a man called "Tubby" Poppleton who hired a horse and dressed it up to look like the Senior Tutor.

5. Try to sustain the fiction that I have heard anything he has said to me over the noise, because I have not, and because he has heard nothing I have said, either, so that by analogy he *knows* I am lying just as surely as I know he is lying.

6. Bend my lips in an attempt to counterfeit a smile unless I am absolutely assured by the raising of a flag with the word JOKE on it that the man has made a joke and not announced that his mother has died.

7. In short, get involved in any more conversations that go:

"I've long been a great admirer of your, er . . . stuff, Mr. . . . er . . . er . . ."

"*How kind of you.*"

"Oh, all kinds."

"*No, I'm afraid some critics haven't been at all kind.*"

"The tall kind? I see. I see."

(A long silence. I think.)

"I particularly liked your last boo . . . er, pla . . ., um, one."

"*Last what?*"

"One."

"*One what?*"

"Um, thing you, well, did."

"*Really? The Press panned it.*"

" 'The Press Bandit'—of course, it was on the tip of my tongue."

"*Well, the Irish banned it.*"

"I mean 'The Irish Bandit', of course. How stupid of me."

"*But everyone else panned it.*"

"Oh, Elsie Pandit. You mean *Mrs.* Pandit?"

"*Who—your missus panned it?*"

"No, India's Mrs. Pandit."

"*They panned it in India, too, did they?*"

"Did they? I suppose Mrs. Pandit banned it."

"*Ah. You know India, do you?*"

"No. You do, do you?"

"*No.*"

"Ah."

"*Hm.*"

(I smile a cryptic, knowing smile. He smiles a cryptic, knowing smile. We are getting on wonderfully. Just then my wife comes up and wants to be introduced, and I have to ask the man who he is.)

Why do I do these things? Do I think the man's going to give me a fiver, or a year's free supply of his works for having heard of his name? Do I think he's going to twist my arm and kick me on the kneecap if I don't like his stuff? He doesn't *expect* me to like it. No one likes it except his wife and the editor of *Spasm* and 780 former pupils of F. R. Leavis. Anyway, I've got him mixed up with someone else, and he didn't do it, and even what he didn't do isn't what I think he did. For heaven's sake, am *I* going to strike *him* because he thinks I'm called Freen, and that I write articles for the Lord's Day Observance Society?

I must not waste my valuable talent for deceit on lies which have no conceivable purpose when I could be saving it up for lies which would show a cash return.

I must instead say "I'm sorry, I didn't quite catch your name."

I must say "I'm sorry, I still haven't quite ..."

I must say "I'm sorry—did you say 'Green' or 'Queen'? Ah. Queen who? Come again ... Queen *Elizabeth*? Elizabeth what?"

I must say "I expect I should know, but I'm afraid I don't—what do you do? I beg your pardon? Rain? You study it, do you—rainfall statistics and so on? No? You rain? You mean you actually rain yourself? I see. I see."

I must say "No, I *don't* see. What do you mean, you rain ...?"

I must ...

I must not, on second thoughts, be pointlessly honest, either. ...

And Home's Son's Father is Hume's Father's Son

What a dynamic start! In the first six days of his ministry Sir Alec Douglas-Home has got rid of an earldom, three lordships, and two baronies; and the new Chancellor of the Duchy of Lancaster and the New Minister of State at the Board of Trade have acquired a viscountcy and a barony respectively.

Meanwhile, at the Conservative Central Office Lord Spoon is trying to drop the Barony of Spoon and pick up the Barony of Bosworth, to complete a set of "Battle" class titles he is collecting. "If I can send in the full set, together with the backs of three old Burke's 'Peerages', I shall win an electric blanket," he told a Press conference late last night.

This vigorous programme cannot, of course, be carried through without some hard rethinking of fundamentals.

At the request of the Garter King-of-Arms, according to the *Daily Telegraph*, the Queen's advisers have been "urgently" considering the question of style and precedence of the former Lord Home's family. A spokesman for the College of Arms told the *Telegraph*: "The question is, for the purpose of precedence, whether the children of peers who have disclaimed are still children of peers."

How the College of Arms faced the problem I don't know, but its rather more venerable rival, the College of Arms and Legges (the name is a corruption of *armorum leges*, the laws of arms), responded with great promptitude. As soon as the urgency and gravity of the question was fully understood, an emergency meeting was called. Members of the College were rushed to London with police escorts, and a jet airliner was specially diverted to bring the Dexter Lord of Legges back from Southern Rhodesia, where he was inspecting pre-war baronetcies for signs of wear.

"Gentlemen," said the Dexter Lord of Legges, "the question is this: Are the children of disclaiming peers still children of peers; and, if not, whose children are they? Would you like to kick off, Rouge Garter Extraordinary?"

Rouge Garter Extraordinary: Well, let's put this question another way. Can commoners whose children are peers' children be in any meaningful sense fathers?

Morte Puissance: Ex nihilo nihil fit. Vide Tollemache v. Tollemache on the strong presumption of non-paternity in the case of an ox that was cited as putative sire of a pig.

Swart Beast: Could not the difficulty be very easily surmounted by requiring peers renouncing their peerages to disclaim the paternity of their children?

Twicester Herald: Then the wife could apply to the courts for a paternity order made out in the name of the extinguished title.

Rouge Garter Extraordinary: The important thing is that these unfortunate children should not be taken away from their homes and put in orphanages unnecessarily.

Morte Puissance: What we must establish here and now, surely, is whether the son of Lord Home (as he then was) is Lord Dunglass (as he now is) or Mr. Douglas-Home junior (as he may well be).

Vray Halidom: Or indeed whether *either* of them is the son of Sir Alec Douglas-Home, or the Earl of Home, or Lord Home, or Lord Hume of Berwick, or Baron Hume of Berwick, or Lord Dunglass, or Baron Douglas of Douglas. As he then was. Or as they then were.

Dexter Lord of Legges: Douglas spelt "Douglas" of Douglas spelt "Douglas"?

Vray Halidom: Precisely so, Legges.

Dexter Lord of Legges: Dashed funny way for a fellow to spell his name.

Swart Beast: Anyway, the permutations are endless.

Rouge Garter Extraordinary: There must be some way of telling. There must be some birthmark or other one of them could produce.

Dexter Lord of Legges: What we must ensure above all is that this unhappy young man is not deprived of someone to call "Father." Or "Lord Father," or "Lord Father of Father," or "Baron Father of Berwick," as the case may be.

Twicester Herald: But my dear Legges, surely Sir Alec, as he now is, could register the titles as a public company— Home, Home, Hume, Hume, Douglas and Dunglass Ltd.—and appoint himself and his son co-directors of it?

Morte Puissance: Would it not be an equally satisfactory solution if the young man's name was spelt "Mr. Douglas-Home" and pronounced "Lord Dunglass"?

Rouge Garter Extraordinary: How about a new title altogether? After all, we must move with the times. I suggest "Lord Dunglass-Home."

Vray Halidom: I like the note of freshness it strikes. And it's obviously an immensely practical little title for running around in. But—well, frankly, it doesn't *speak* to me.

Dexter of Legges: Beast?

Swart Beast: Well, for my money I don't think you can beat "Lord Douglas-Dunglass." There's a tremendously rugged integrity about that title. It's a valid response—a nexus of creative outgoingness—what I might call an essentially dynamic act of awareness. Also the hyphen takes out for cleaning.

Morte Puissance: I'm prepared to go some way with Beast. But when it comes to sheer, solid craftsmanship, give me a good old-fashioned title like "Lord Douglas, or, As You Like It."

Rouge Garter Extraordinary: Preferably pronounced "Lord Dunglass, or, What You Will."

Vray Halidom: Well, I think, you'd have to go a long way to beat Lord Home Number Fifteen, in B Flat Minor.

Swart Beast: Or the sheer sensual awareness of "The Rokeby Douglas."

Morte Puissance: May I put in a word for "On Hearing the First Dunglass of Spring"?

Dexter Lord of Legges: Well, there we were, then. The team can't make up its mind whether former peers' children are peers' children or not. But we're all agreed that a rose by any other name smells just like a rose, a ruse, a rouglas, or a runglass, as the case may be.

Ron Number

Whatever other unseen beings we do or do not believe in, we are all believers in Ron Number. Ron Number is mysterious, unpredictable, unknowable. But undeniably, Ron Number is.

He speaks to us all at one time or another, and when he speaks, there is no denying the call. The telephone rings. "R E Pugnance 4278," one says. "Oh," replies the voice, "Ron Number." And rings off.

Ron Number never forgets us. He speaks to us on our birthdays; at Candlemas, Martinmas, Lammastide, and Septuagesima. He remembers us on Mondays. He remembers us on Tuesdays. He remembers us on Wednesdays, Thursdays, and Fridays. He does not forget us at the weekend.

He calls us when we least expect it—saving us from the tedium of being asleep at six o'clock in the morning and interrupting our idle reverie as we sit in the lavatory. When one's guests have been warmed with food and wine to the point where they are just beginning to speak openly and directly from the depths of themselves, Ron Number phones. "Oh," he says, "Ron Number." And afterwards nothing is quite the same again.

What is Ron Number trying to tell us? His utterances are oblique and cryptic. I have humbly recorded the ones vouchsafed to me in the Book of Ron Number, which in the Improved Version comes between the Book of Usually Reliable Sources and the Book of Celebrities. Here is a reading from Ron Number, vii 3–10 as a sample:

"And when the bell chymed, he made answer according to the law and to the usage of his house, saying: 'REPugnance 4278.' And Ron Number spake unto him, saying: 'Oh.' And Ron Number spake further with him saying: 'Ron Number.' And Ron Number here made an end to his speaking.

"And on another occasion Ron Number spake unto him saying: 'Oh. Oh.'

"And at another chyming of the bell Ron Number saith: 'Oh, terribly sorry.'

"And at another: 'Terribly sorry. Frightfully sorry.'

"And at another: 'I wish to speak to Mr. Chatterjee, in the small room on the first floor.'

"And at another: 'Is that REPugnance 4728? That's right—4728. That's what I said—4728. Yes, 47...—oh, 4278? Oh. Sorry.'

"And at another Ron Number saith nothing, but silently departed. Yet was he known even by his silence."

A great deal, of course, has been written by commentators attempting to elucidate these utterances. Most commentators have pointed to the remarkable insistence on a sense of grief for transgression. Others have pointed out that the sum of 4278 and 4728 is exactly 9006. Some have seen the mysterious Mr. Chatterjee as a textual corruption of Mt. Chimborazo.

Almost everyone has been struck by the constant repetition of "Oh," or "O." A minority of somewhat eccentric commentators have taken this to be a revelation of the Golden Number, and have attempted to use the figure zero to compute the date of the invention of the telephone. The usual interpretation up to now has been that it stood for Operator, and was intended as giving a metaphorical corporeal identity to Ron Number to make him comprehensible to the human intelligence. But the most modern commentators read the whole phrase as "O Ron Number!" and regard Ron Number as a self-worshipping entity, a sort of abstraction inherent in the telephone system.

One day, almost all of us more or less believe, Ron Number will come in person. He will ring the front-door bell. "Oh, Ron Number," he will say, and stand there mysterious and awful, the miraculous visual equivalent of the universal way he sounds, as he speaks with the tongues of old ladies, wizened Chinamen, fat company directors, and burly West Indians.

Not, of course, that Ron Numberism is entirely undivided in its beliefs. There is, for example, a sect of telephone subscribers in Bexleyheath, the principal tenet of whose creed seems to be that I am an incarnation of the South Eastern Gas Board.

They ring me up and pray to me. "Oh, South Eastern Gas Board?" ask the more agnostic members of the faith, sceptically. "O South Eastern Gas Board!" the true believers proclaim in resounding vocatives.

As an orthodox Ron Numberist I try to put them right. But you can't combat faith with reason, and the really convinced believers go right ahead and pray to me to heal a sick gas water heater, or provide them with a refrigerator, or even sometimes to take from them an old and ailing gas cooker.

Perhaps they are sustained in their faith by a miracle—a time when after earnest prayers had been offered up to REPugnance 4278 a palsied gas water heater suddenly and wondrously filled with gas and blew up, killing seven. Perhaps they have a chapel of their own, and a wise old preacher who tells them that if when they phone REPugnance 4278 they imagine

63

they hear someone denying that RE Pugnance 4278 is the South Eastern Gas Board it is only a temptation put in their way to test their faith, and that they should strengthen themselves to overcome it by telephoning twice as often. Perhaps they sing simple gas hymns, like:

> Oh how the weary heart desires
> The golden streets, the pearly gate,
> The gaseous heaven of the wires—
> RE Pugnance 4278.

Only, of course, an argument breaks out as to whether the number is 4278 or 4872, and a schism occurs. But the more schisms they have the better; the more combinations of numbers they try the more people to whom they will have to say "Oh, Ron Number." Yes, whatever our beliefs, and whether we know it or not, we are all doing Ron Number's work.

The Sad Tale of P-t-r B-nnykin

Once upon a time there was a naughty little rabbit called Peter Bunnykin.

This sentence is almost certainly actionable (noted Mr. K. J. Writweather, barrister-at-law and libel-reader for *Chicks' Own*, in the margin of the galley-proof) unless we are absolutely certain that Mr. Bunnykin is no longer alive.

"Naughty" is indefensible, and I think to be on the safe side we should also remove the name, since a jury might conceivably hold that calling Mr. Bunnykin "a little rabbit" was damaging.

Even so, Mr. Bunnykin might be able to show that the phrase "a little rabbit" identified him to those who knew him, and I should feel happier if it were removed. If you think "Once upon a time there was," is not strong enough as an opening sentence on its own I should be prepared to accept a completely fictitious description—"a big griffin," say, or "a medium-sized dodo."

64

Peter Bunnykin lived in a cosy little rabbit-hole in Bluebell Woods.

Any hole in the ground, however innocent it seems, may, unknown to the author, be a Regional Seat of Government, and as such covered by D-notices. I suggest: "He lived in a cosy little dwelling in a wooded location."

One day he decided to go along to Farmer Barleycorn's lettuce-patch and steal a lettuce.

This imputation upon the good faith of Mr. Bunnykin's intentions would be impossible to substantiate. Either "steal" must be changed to "purchase," or else the link with Mr. Bunnykin must be weakened by changing the sentence to "Later, a rabbit went to Farmer Barleycorn's lettuce-patch, etc." Then if Mr. Bunnykin ever did bring a case I think it could be argued with some success that it was never intended to suggest that the rabbit who took the lettuce was the same rabbit that was mentioned earlier.

Off he went, hippity-hop, hippity-hop.

I suppose this might just pass as fair comment.

With two snip-snaps of his little front teeth he was through the fence around the lettuce-patch.

I suggest: "At another point, a rabbit was in the lettuce-patch." By the sound of it, an action may well lie against the manufacturers of the fencing material, and by the time this story is in print the whole matter may be *sub judice*.

What a bad rabbit he was!

The nearest I can get to preserving the rhythm of this sentence and avoiding any resetting is "What a brown rabbit he was!" I realise this is not very close to the original sense. The best I can do in that direction is "What a broad-minded rabbit he was!"

But he had eaten only two lettuces when Farmer Barleycorn leapt out from behind a hedge and gave him a terrible spanking!

"But only two lettuces had been eaten . . ."—the passive is in general a much less dangerous voice—"But only two lettuces had been eaten when a rabbit and a hand were in collision."

And Farmer Barleycorn said; "It's not the first time I've caught you stealing my lettuces, young Peter Bunnykin."

I think the nearest we can get here, if you are prepared to

65

take a calculated risk, is "Farmer Barleycorn then made a statement."

But coming on top of everything else I'm afraid there is still an element of innuendo even in this. I must admit I should feel safer if it was changed to "Someone said something." Though here again we must ask ourselves, as always, "Will he sue?" I'm afraid that in my experience *someone* always sues. I should sleep easier if we changed it to "No one said something," or better still, "No one said nothing."

Poor Peter Bunnykin slunk off home with his tail between his legs, feeling very small and wishing the earth would swallow him up.

I have as you suggested taken the opinion of leading counsel on this passage, and the more we discussed it, the more ways we could see in which it could be taken to be tendentious. Adding together all our reservations, we suggest: "A certain animal went home in a certain manner, with his tail in a certain position, feeling a certain size, and wishing that a certain object would perform a certain action."

And so Peter Bunnykin lived happily ever after, with a permanent house-guest who was a model with plenty of men-friends: his name connected with members of the Royal Family in vile rumours published by scandal-mongering children's comics on the Continent: being frequently helped home in a state of collapse after gay parties suffering from influenza: with a trunkful of letters from the Under-Secretary for Rabbit Affairs addressing him as "My dear Bunnykin": and described by a Divorce Court judge as a thoroughly rotten, contemptible little rabbit without a single spark of common decency.

This bit seems more or less all right.

Sir,—We are instructed on behalf of our client Mr. Lybell Laws, whose attention has been drawn to an article containing certain extremely damaging innuendoes....

Fog-like Sensations

(According to some sympathisers, the reason why drivers on the motorways failed to slow down in thick fog recently, and so crashed into each other in multiple collisions of up to thirty vehicles, was simply because the authorities had failed to provide illuminated signs explaining that the fog was fog. This is a situation on which Wittgenstein made one or two helpful remarks in a previously unpublished section of "Philosophical Investigations".)

694. Someone says, with every sign of bewilderment (wrinkled forehead, widened eyes, an anxious set to the mouth): "I do not know there is fog on the road unless it is accompanied by an illuminated sign saying 'fog'."

When we hear this, we feel dizzy. We experience the sort of sensations that go with meeting an old friend one believed was dead. I want to say: "But *this* is the man philosophers are always telling us about! This is the man who does not understand—the man who goes on asking for explanations after everything has been explained!"

(A sort of Socratic Oliver Twist. Compare the feelings one would have on meeting Oliver Twist in the flesh. "And now I want you to meet Oliver Twist."—"But ...!")

695. Now I feel a different sort of excitement. I see in a flash a thought forming as it were before my mind's eye—"This is at last the sort of situation which philosophers have always waited for—the sort of situation in which one as a philosopher can offer practical help!"

696. Imagine that the motorist said: "The trouble is, I can't see the fog for the fog." We might understand this as a request for *practical* information, and try to answer it by showing him the definition of "fog" in the dictionary. To this he might reply: "I can't see 'fog' for the fog." We respond by putting the

dictionary an inch in front of his eyes. Now he says: "I can't see the fog for 'fog'."

697. At this point a philosopher might want to say: "He sees the fog but he does not perceive its fogginess." Ask yourself what could possibly be the object of saying this.

698. Now the man says: "I can see the fog perfectly well, but I don't know that it's fog." I feel an urge to say: "Yet you know it's fog that you don't know to be fog!" (The deceptively normal air of paradoxes.) One can imagine his replying: "Naturally—it looks like fog." Or, if he is familiar with philosophical language: "Of course—I know that I am having fog-like sensations." And if one asked him what he meant by *that*, perhaps he would say: "It looks like what I see in places where I should know what I was seeing if it were labelled 'fog'."

699. *Now* the feeling of dizziness vanishes. We feel we want to say: "Now it seems more like a dull throbbing behind the eyes."

700. Of course, one is familiar with the experience of seeing something ambiguous. "Now it is the Taj Mahal—now it is fog." And one can imagine having a procedural rule that anything ambiguous should be treated as the Taj Mahal unless we see that it is labelled "fog."

701. The motorist replies: "What sort of rule is this? Surely the best guarantee I can have that the fog is fog is if I fail to see the sign saying 'fog' because of the fog."—One can imagine uses for the rule. For example, to lure people to their deaths.

702. Still the man seems uneasy. "To be sure that the fog is fog because it is labelled 'fog', I must first be sure that 'fog' is 'fog'. Now, supposing, without its being perceptible to the naked eye, the top of the 'o' were slightly open. How am I to be certain that it could not be accepted as a 'u', so that the word was not 'fog' at all but 'fug'? Or how can I be certain that the first letter is really 'f' and not a grossly deformed but still meaningful 'b'?"

So now we have to have a label for "fog"! And another label for the label of "fog"!

703. But we are not yet out of the wood! (Or, as one might say, out of the fog.) The motorist might object: "I *still* cannot understand. I see that the fog is labelled 'fog', and that 'fog' is

68

labelled ' "fog" ', and so forth. But how am I to know that 'fog' *means* fog, or that ' "fog" ' *means* 'fog'?"

So we must qualify still further. We must expand "fog" to read " 'fog', where 'fog' means fog."

704. Now imagine the motorist's face. Imagine that the doubtful expression remains. Imagine that he says: "But how do I know that the expression ' "fog", where "fog" means fog' means ' "fog", where "fog" means fog' "?

705. What sort of game are we playing here? What sort of language are we using? I am tempted to ask, what sort of man am I being used by? I have a certain feeling that goes with grating teeth, a frown, flushed cheeks. I want to say: "My offer of help is being abused."

706. One might try to provide the man with a mental picture, a working model of his position—as it were a map to enable him to get his bearings. I might say: "You are in a complete mental fog about the whole business." He seizes on this eagerly. He goes through the motions of assenting—nodding his head, pursing his lips, saying: "Yes, yes, that's it exactly. I am in a complete mental fog."

Now one asks: "But how do you *know* it's a mental fog you're in?"

707. At once he cries: "NOW I see! I see that I don't know I'm in a mental fog at all! I need an illuminated mental sign saying 'mental fog'."

708. If a lion could speak, it would not understand itself.

Dig My Dogma

"If you don't 'dig' dogma," said an advertisement for a religious magazine in *The Times* this week, "you should certainly 'get with' the current issue of *Prism*. The first five contributions concern themselves with John Robinson's 'Honest to God,' and concern themselves with it very deeply. To the agnostic who wrote this advertisement they were intensely stimulating and revealing reading. . . ."

The agnostic whose services were retained by *Prism* to

testify to the stimulating qualities of their theology does not reveal his identity. A pity. The astigmatic who wrote this article (his name can be inspected on request at our Erith works) has gone into the advertisement pretty deeply and would have liked to congratulate him on a stimulating and intensely revealing piece of work.

Not to mince words, I thought it was a unique combination of getwithery and godwottery. Or to put it another way, an exquisite blend of dogma and digma. In fact I thought it was the most stimulating and revealing bit of devotional prose published on the subject of John Robinson—known to millions of ordinary religion-lovers as Jack Woolwich—since Mike Canterbury said he was "specially grieved" because Jack had published his views in a newspaper article which was, among other things, "crystal clear in its arguments."

Most stimulating and revealing of all was the advertiser's basic idea of getting an agnostic to write the testimonial. It amazes me that Christians didn't think of this earlier. ("To the agnostic who wrote this gospel, the events narrated seem verily 'far out'—but wondrously 'swinging' none the less.") I hope they will appoint a panel of neutral agnostic advisers to go right through the Thirty-Nine Articles from beginning to end and sort out the stimulating from the unstimulating.

It would certainly be in line with the most enlightened modern practice as I have come to know it. Almost every single article I have ever written on the subject of religious belief has subsequently been either commended or reprinted by some religious publication. I'm not entirely sure with what motive the other cheek is not only turned but so relentlessly hammered against one's fist. But I have an uneasy mental picture of a procession, like the terrible band of medieval flagellants in "The Seventh Seal," crawling across modern England on their knees, grinning with horrible pleasure as they scourge one another with anti-religious satire and blasphemous jokes, bearing aloft images of broad minds, and crying "*Like* us. *Please* like us!"

"May I say how much I'm enjoying this article?" writes the Bishop of Twicester. "I shall certainly take your tip and reprint it, if I may, in my *Diocesan News*, in a section we have entitled 'The Other Chap's Point of View.'

"There's nothing I enjoy more than having my leg pulled—
the harder the better! I'm sure God enjoys it, too—though of
course the question of whether His Leg exists to be pulled is
one which, as you have shown in your amusing articles, we
mustn't take for granted too complacently!

"You're absolutely right, of course. We are, alas, sometimes
tempted to curry public favour. But it is also true that the best
way to protect one's most cherished convictions is not always
to stand rigid against the enemy and be cut down, but to smile
and co-operate with him. I think some of us are discovering
that the Vicar of Bray was not as 'square' as he has sometimes
been painted!

"After all, if we go some way to meet you chaps, you can
scarcely help but come some way to meet us! Such is human
nature. I saw in the paper the other day David Frost saying that
after one of his little religious skits which had offended some
people he went to church—and the sidesman told him how
much he had enjoyed the programme. One concession calls
forth another, you see. I myself had an interesting chat with
Ken Nocker after that delightful take-off he did of the
Crucifixion, and he told me that it was only the commercial
aspects of it he was against really.

"It used to be rock-and-roll singers we found ourselves
entirely in agreement with, and then it was teenage satirists.
Now it's agnostic copy-writers. Of course, it's a good thing for
all of us—it helps to keep our minds open and flexible.

"One of the most encouraging things about the age we live in
is this ability not to take ourselves too seriously. There's no
harm in behaving like men of the world, after all, and I like to
think that we can all enjoy a joke and a prayer together,
whichever side of the fence we are on.

"I dare say you'll satirise this letter! It might deserve it, too,
for all I know. More power to your elbow—I thoroughly
enjoy having my complacency shattered!"

The Mails Must Go Through

Dear Joyce,

Just a line to say thank you for your letter. Lots of news to tell you, but must rush, so excuse scrawl.

I hope you and Howard are keeping well, and that Nicholas and Simonetta are in "rude health." Dominic and Nicolette are both "blooming". They've got through the summer with no coughs or sneezes so far, though I suppose there's plenty of time yet, so we're "keeping our fingers crossed!" John sends his love. Had a letter from Ida on Monday—she and Ralph are both well. She asks to be remembered to you, and says Simon and Nicola are both "blooming." Ralph sends his love.

Well, I must stop rambling on like this or I will go on all night. Must rush to catch the post.

All my love,

Eileen

Dear Eileen,

I expect you will almost faint with surprise to find your ever-loving sister-in-law replying already! Wonders will never cease. The trouble is you're such a virtuous correspondent you make a girl feel the still, small voice pricking away like mad! Wild horses couldn't drag me to take up pen and paper normally, but Duty calls!

Glad to hear Dominic and Nicolette are blossoming. Nicholas and Simonetta are disgustingly healthy, needless to say. Also had a letter from Ida (not usually the world's greatest correspondent, so you see the age of miracles is not past!), and she says Simon and Nicola are flourishing like the proverbial green bay tree. She and Ralph send you their love. Howard sends his love too of course.

Forgive the horrible scrawl. Lots more to tell, but must stop now or shall have to go over on to new page, and it's not worth it just for a line or two.

All my love,

Joyce

Dear Joyce,
    Just a line to thank you for your letter. Been meaning to write ever since it arrived last Wednesday (first post), but I've been putting it off and putting it off, you know how it is. I feel very guilty for not "doing my duty" more promptly, but I always was a poor correspondent. Somehow I never seem to have the time—I expect you find it much the same. How you manage to keep it up I simply do not know. I suppose some people are just "born" letter-writers! Not me, worse luck, it's a terrible chore.
    Dominic and Nicolette are very well—no coughs or sneezes so far, touch wood. Ralph and Ida were over here with Simon and Nicola—all in the "pink." They send their love. How are Nicholas and Simonetta?
    Well, I mustn't go on, I'm just indulging myself. I must rush, or you won't get this first post. Please excuse scrawl.

All my love,

Eileen

Dear Eileen,
    Don't faint with surprise, but it really is a letter from me. Wonders will never cease. Give a girl the prize. Believe it or not, I feel the stern call of Duty sometimes! I'm quite the little model correspondent—I must be shamed into it by your sterling example! I feel sorry for you having to decipher yet another dollop of my famous horrible scrawl, but on your own head be it—don't say I didn't warn you!
    First and foremost, I had a letter from Ida (yes, you did hear right!). Ralph sends his love, and apparently Simon and Nicola are both A1 at Lloyd's. I trust Dominic and Nicolette are likewise and ditto. Nicholas and Simonetta I am glad to inform you are their usual sweet (ha, ha!) selves. Howard sends his love.
    Well, the bottom of the page is already raising its ugly head,

73

so I must restrain what Howard calls my boundless gift for gossip, and dash to catch the post.

All my love,

Joyce

P S. *Must go over on to a new page to tell you—so funny. Had an extraordinary epistle from Our Mutual Mum-in-law—rambling on about everything under the sun from French history to politics. Yes,* politics, *for heaven's sake, in a letter! I didn't read it all, of course, but the general gist of it seemed to be that she was well and sent her love.*

Dear Joyce,

Just a line "in haste" to apologise for not writing before, so excuse the scrawl. Keep promising myself I'll sit down and write you a really good long letter one of these days, but never seem to get the chance. You're such a good letter-writer it makes me feel ashamed of my own poor efforts. I suppose it's the way you "put" things. I always feel "I wish I'd thought of that"—but then you've got the gift, haven't you? When I sit down to write it all flies out of my head. But one of these days I really will sit down and write a good long letter.

Well, sorry to have "gone on" so long—I never "know when to stop," that's my trouble. Must rush to catch post, so I'm afraid I'll have to close.

All my love,

Eileen

P S. Knew there was something I meant to say—everyone is well and sends their love.

Oh, Un Peu, Vous Savez, Un Peu

Considering how much at home middle-class intellectuals like you and me feel in the presence of the middle-class intellectuals from the rest of Europe we meet on holiday, it's astonishing how little we can actually communicate. Or, to put it another way, considering the ratio of effort to information in those long holiday sessions of laboured English or paraplegic French, it's amazing we can go on seeing ourselves as having that broad understanding of the world we feel so comfortably in the abstract.

It's different for the spying classes, of course. If the novels do not lie, any plain English spy having difficulties in Bulgaria, say, finds that the smattering of Bulgarian he picked up from collecting stamps as a boy is quite adequate for passing himself off as a used horse dealer from Plovdiv. And when in Chapter 16 he finds himself in the clutches of the notorious Bulgarian police chief, Colonel Khaskovo, communication doesn't falter for an instant.

"So, my friend," says Khaskovo in beautifully starched English, "your foolish inquisitiveness has necessitated our taking certain precautions. It grieves me deeply, believe me, that you will unfortunately not be in a position to appreciate the full fiendish ingenuity with which your so clumsy blunderings will be brought to an end."

How different it all is when the kindly-looking lady at the next table in the *pensione*, whom one for some reason takes to be a German, tries to establish some elementary communication by showing a polite interest in one's child. Taking one to be French, she remarks:

"Quel âge?"

In any other circumstances the phrase would be transparently comprehensible. But somehow, spoken in an Italian *pensione* by a woman one takes to be German, a curious obscurity hangs over it. Kellarzh? Kellarzh? Ah, I see— "Qu'elle large!"—obviously Teutonic pidgin French for "How wide she is!"

"Er, ja," one says, tactfully helping the poor soul back into her native language.

"Jahr? Ein Jahr?"

"Ja. Er, ja."

"Ein Jahr! Fantastisch!"

"Oh, *Jahr*. Er, nein Jahr. I mean...."

"*Nine* Jahr? Neun year?"

"Oh, nein, nein!"

75

"Neun Monat? Neuf mois?"

"Nein nine! I mean, nein neun. Nicht nein—er, neun. Er, excuse me—ich muss à la plage, er, gehen."

Of course, one gets beyond this stage, because the woman and her husband (who are in fact Psychomanian) turn out to speak quite good English. But the further one gets beyond, the heavier the going becomes. For one curious thing, they admire and wish to discuss a whole Pantheon of famous Englishmen of whom one has never oneself heard.

What do we think of Spencer Philips, the philosopher? Oh, really? In their country he is *very* widely read. How privileged we are to belong to the nation that has produced Gordon Roberts, the great modern dramatist, and Philip Gordons, the celebrated novelist. *No?* In their country even the children read translations of them. We shall be saying next that we have never heard of Gordon Spencer, the sociologist, or the world-famous Spencer Roberts, whose political writings have had such an influence on modern Psychomanian thinking!

One tries to return the national compliment, by expressing one's admiration for that grand old man of Psychomanian letters, Sigismund Cortex. Or does one mean Siegfried Catalept? Either way they haven't heard of him.

Worse, whatever level a conversation starts on, it soon comes sprawling down among an unavoidable undergrowth of explanation and counter-explanation. One may start by talking about the ethical well-springs of government, say, but within minutes one is down with one's face in this sort of mud:

"Ah, I must explain. In our country, in each small part of land we have committee governing. What is this called in English?"

"Rural district councils, perhaps?"

"Rura distry council. Yes. In each divided part of land is rura distry council. But in the towns also is rura distry council."

"No, in the towns we call them urban district councils. Or do I mean borough councils?"

"Yes. Of course, the urban distry councils are the underdogs—idiomatic word I learned—the underdogs of the rura distry councils."

"Oh, no."

"In our country oh yes. In our country in the country—can

76

I say that?—is also what you call *country* councils. But I think our country councils are not just the same as your country councils. I must explain...."

I sometimes wonder if Colonel Khaskovo and his friend were correctly reported. What the dreaded Bulgarian police chief really said, I suspect, in the confusion of at last confronting the British master-spy in the secret atomic pile was:

"Mein Gott! Wer ist dies?"

"Wer?" repeats the British master of espionage stupidly, his grasp of German interrogative pronouns slipping somewhat in the stress of the moment. "Dies ist die Pile."

"D. Pile?" repeats the Colonel, momentarily taken aback. "Nicht J. Standish, of British Intelligence?"

"Oh, who, ich?"

"O. Whuish or J. Standish—is no matter. Lay down your arms and put up your arms. Can I say that?"

"Hands."

"Ah, hands, yes. I must explain. I have a firehand here, and if you are not putting up your arms I will pull the—what is in English the little thing hereunder which when one is pulling it makes bang bang...?"

Yes, as our wonderful English poet Markson Spencers said: North is north and south is south: They can only talk with their foot in their mouth.

Total Scholarship

I was delighted to hear
I was depressed to see
I was interested to learn that the complete works of the late Charlie Parker, the great master of modern jazz, are being brought out in a variorum edition, including all the false starts and alternative readings.

It surprises me
It does not surprise me
It surprises me that no one has yet suggested publishing a

variorum edition of any journalist's works. I should think they must get round to it finally.

As a matter of fact, I have given the matter a certain amount / a great deal of thought, and I am rather inclined / absolutely resolved to make a start in that direction myself. For the benefit of posterity I am going to begin writing my own footnotes.[1] I'm going to stop / cease / desist from crossing out the speeling[2] mistakes, and thoughtlessly chucking / casually flinging / irresponsibly precipitating the material I don't use into the waste-paper basket.[3] In a word, I'm going to compile my *own* ~~voriarum~~[4] ~~viarorum~~[5] variorum edition. It'll save somebody[6] a lot of work, anyway.

James Thurber[7] once remarked that if you saw his first drafts you'd think the cleaning woman[8] had written them. If his first drafts really could have provoked scholars to suppose anything so stimulating to literary research, they were source-material which it was wanton vandalism of Thurber to throw away.[9] DON'T FORGET RING CRUMBLE ABOUT DINNER THURS*!!!*[10]

This new approach represents a serious criticism of our recieved (check spelling)[11] idea of the function of art. From a superficial point of view, it has always seemed that the whole

[1] This is a good example of the *genre*.
[2] Mis-spelling for *spieling*—"persuasive talking."
[3] Reichart remarks that "basket" was a common euphemism in the Royal Navy *c*.1930 for "bastard," and suggests that by analogy with debased Anglo-Indian usages such as "janker-wallah" the phrase "waste-paper basket" may perhaps be understood as "salvage collector." But more probably in this context, "a receptacle for waste-paper."
[4] *Voriarum:* corruption of *vomitorium*.
[5] *Viarorum:* i.e., via Rorum. Rorum is a non-existent place, therefore, "by way of nowhere," i.e., "not by any means" (humorous usage).
[6] Exactly whom is a matter of speculation. Reichart suggests that he himself is intended here, but Skimming disputes this.
[7] James Grover Thurber (1894–1961).
[8] The so-called "Dark Lady of the Broom Cupboard." Identified by Skimming as Della (cf. Thurber: "My World and Welcome To It"). Pilsudsky's theory that it was the Earl of Arran is not generally accepted.
[9] Probably intended jocularly, but the simple truth none the less.
[10] Meaning obscure. For an interesting explanation in Jungian terms, see Rosie (Journ. of Amer. Soc. of Ephem. Lit., vol XXIII).
[11] It is typical of the author's "feel" for language that he sensed this word was mis-spelt.

78

point of books, articles, poems, and so forth was their form and subject.[12] It has been left to modern scholarship to show that their real significance lies in the light which they cast upon their authors.

In other words

To put it slightly differently

Otherwise speaking (Is this English?)[13] a creative undertaking is nothing less than the autobiography of the undertak

That is to say, art is interesting because it tells us about the artists[14]—who are of course interesting because they produce ar

In other words, the whole of art is nothing less than a running gossip column on the art world.[15]

What the Peepers See

A perpetual state of conflict and unrest exists between my eyes and the printed word. To be blunt, my eyes do not find words congenial co-workers in the business of communication.

It's not the fault of the words, which are patient and long-suffering in the face of constant abuse. It's my eyes. They won't settle down to do one job at a time; they're slapdash; they jump to conclusions; and they're highly counter-suggestible. Speaking for the management, I can tell you they're a right pair of layabouts.

They read MACMILLAN PUTS PARTY'S TRUST IN HOME as MACMILLAN PUT PARTLY TRUSSED IN HOME. With salacious agility they leapt five paragraphs of life-enhancing descriptive prose to the erotic events they have miraculously detected at the bottom of the next page.

[12] This observation has been confirmed by many other authorities, e.g. Westland, Boosey, Sidgwick, Fanfani and da Costa.
[13] No.
[14] Very true.
[15] This pungent and devastating conclusion is of the greatest interest because of the light it sheds on the author's ability to reach, in this case, a pungent and devastating conclusion.

They read magazines backwards, jumping unsteadily back through the country notes and the annual reports of holding company holding companies, and give out exhausted long before they reach MIXED MANNING: A CAUTIOUS RE-ASSESSMENT? at the front.

They're at their very worst with the eight daily newspapers that face them each morning. The rich profusion of sizes and styles and arrangements exhibited by the words in the news-papers completely demoralises them. They run hopelessly back and forth from one story to another like panic-stricken chickens. And yet they're so hidebound by restrictive practices that even at this juncture they refuse to see more than one size of type at a time—if they see the small headlines they don't see the large ones, and if they see the text they don't see the headlines at all.

Heavens, it makes me mad to think of all the time and ingenuity the printers and sub-editors have expended to make life easy for the readers' eyes—only to have ungrateful young peepers like mine pick and choose and complain. But isn't that the modern pupil all over? All they think of is eye, eye, eye.

With typical cowardly idleness they always start by picking on the smallest type at the bottom of the page, hoping no doubt that my hand will absent-mindedly turn the page over before they come up against anything their own size.

Short of pinning the newspaper to the wall, and slowly advancing from the other side of the room with my glasses off, reading it line by line like an oculist's chart, I suppose I'm condemned to go on starting the front page each morning with the *This Funny Old World* section at the bottom:

HIS PET ATE—TROUSERS

Harold Morbidly (47) went to work in his underpants after his pet hamster, Lulu, ate his trousers, Chingford, Essex, magistrates were told yesterday.

Discouraged by this inauspicious intelligence, my eyes labour slowly up from the bottom of the next column along.

Last night a man was helping the police in their inquiries.
"I tried to stop him," said Mrs. Sough, "by running after him shouting 'Help, police!'"

He grabbed the money from the till and ran out of the shop. Then he pulled out a gun and said, "This is a stick-up."

"So of course," said Mrs. Sough, "I assumed he was a perfectly ordinary customer...."

It doesn't make any sense to me. Hey, just a moment—didn't I catch a glimpse of "intimacy occurred" seven columns over to the left somewhere? Ah, here we are.

... An opportunity to show that the Prime Minister knew the North-East with considerable intimacy occurred when....

Oh. H'm. Where was I?

"The morals of young people today," said Sir Harold Sidewinder...

That wasn't it, was it?

... are to be either scrapped or put into mothballs.

Nor that. Where the devil was it?

HEAVY LASSES KEEP GIANT COMPANY IN BED

No.

"The morals of young people..."

What? Heavy lasses do *what?* Where did I see that? Oh, HEAVY LOSSES KEEP GIANT COMPANY IN RED. Yes. Heavens, I'm bored. Must try and stagger a bit higher, though.

... wiped out. First reports put the number of dead and missing at...

Funny about those heavy lasses, I must say.

... when disaster struck ... many thousands rendered homeless...

What was that rather amusing story about a hamster going into mothballs? Forgotten already. More or less squeezed this page dry, haven't I? Just glance at the main headline...

WAR DECLARED

...and I can turn over. Nothing.in the damned paper, as usual.

I don't know what the solution is. Perhaps lead the page with HAMSTER INCIDENT SHOCK and make the tailpiece at the bottom

Page One Fun

WELL, I DECLARE ...!

"I declare war on Russia," said Sir Alec Douglas-Home (60) opening a Staggered Hours exhibition yesterday. Experts combing the radio-active rubble of London last night believed that what Sir Alec really said was not "Russia" but "rush-hour."

My eyes would get round it somehow, though. Probably start reading the *advertisements*.

On the Subject of Objects

I expect you're pretty used to people lying here in your consulting-room and telling you the most terrible things about themselves, aren't you, Dr. Wienerkreis? I mean, thinking they've got all sorts of frightful things wrong with them which turn out to be nothing but...?

Yes, well, anyway, the point is, Dr. Wienerkreis, I'm suffering from, I mean, I think I might possibly have got a... well, *a serendipity deficiency*.

I mean, I never *find* things. Everyone I know but me seems to find things. What sort of things? Well, they find, sort of, *objects*. They come across fantastic sea-shells on the beach. They stumble on oddly shaped pieces of wood in fields. They glance into a junk shop and pick up an elegant brass letter balance for seven-and-six, say, or an amusing Victorian steel engraving for tenpence-halfpenny. Well, you know, *objects*.

What? Well, they take them home and arrange them as it were casually in their living-rooms. What do they do then? Well, I suppose they look at them. I mean, they're intriguing things. I suppose they look at them and feel intrigued. When they have guests the guests look at them and feel intrigued.

For example, we have some friends called the Crumbles. When one goes into the Crumbles' living-room one's surrounded on all sides by patch-boxes, astrolabes, sticks of Victorian rock, model Dreadnoughts, lumps of quartz-porphyry, eighteenth-century milking stools, Chinese tooth-picks. One's intrigued. It gives one something to talk about.

What does one say? Well, I don't know, one says perhaps *"What's this intriguing little object, then?"* Something like that. And Christopher Crumble says, more or less, *"That? Oh, that's an early Georgian dentist's forceps I found by sheerest chance at a little shop I know down in Devizes."* Or something along those lines. Well, then you're away on a sort of whimsical-cultural, or cultural-whimsical, conversation that will see you through until the soup's on the table.

I know, I know.... Of course I don't think *everyone* collects intriguing objects. Some people collect beer-mats and miniature liqueur bottles. Some people collect Louis XV candle-snuffers or Baroque door-knobs. But the people I know are too sophisticated for beer-mats and too poor for Baroque door-knobs. So they collect amusing objects. The point is, Dr. Wienerkreis, I have a social context I have to try to fit into.

The trouble is, the fields I walk through are just full of earth. Whenever I look into a junk shop the contents consist exclusively of junk. I never see any amusing Victorian ship's chronometers. All I see is heaps of rusty ice-skates, broken clockwork trains, warped rattan cake-stands, and chipped mauve cocktail sets that someone got for 1,700 cigarette tokens in 1938. The only thing I've ever found anywhere is the word *serendipity*, which I came across by absolute chance in a little dictionary I know....

Yes, of course it matters. When the Crumbles come to dinner with us they're surrounded by great quantities of nothing. Yes, nothing at all. Well, to be absolutely precise, I suppose there are usually a few things lying around like plastic giveaways out of cereal packets, week-old copies of the *Daily*

Mirror, broken sunglasses, bits of paper with "No milk Sunday" written on them, that sort of thing.

I mean, our living-room is a cultural desert. You can't expect people to say "*Where did you get this intriguing little 'Daily Mirror' from?*" You can't show guests the plastic television personalities, and explain how you just picked them up by sheerest chance as they fell out of a little Fungles packet you know down behind the refrigerator.

Of course, the plastic television personalities may come to be amusing objects in time. By the turn of the century the graciously ageing Crumbles may well have a small but distinguished collection of them in their living-room, together with an amusing old wireless valve, a highly intriguing Dun-in-a-Jiff patent potato peeler (c. 1960), and a number of nostalgically beautiful and rather valuable photographs from *Reveille* of *le pin-up de che secake* school. Not us, though—we'll just have a couple of week-old numbers of the *Times-Mirror* and some broken bits of the central-heating reactor lying on the floor.

I need help, Dr. Wienerkreis. Help myself? You mean, practise? Start off modestly and work up to normal serendipity by easy stages?

I see what you mean. I could begin by arranging the old *Daily Mirrors* and the broken sunglasses in a tasteful way. Is that the sort of thing you have in mind? Then I could try finding slightly unusual looking pebbles and bits of twig. I could buy some of the less rusty ice-skates and the less chipped mauve cocktail-shakers. Then I could gradually work back through 1930s toothbrush-holders, 1920s false teeth, and Edwardian rubber dog-bones, to Diamond Jubilee shoe-trees and Great Exhibition bradawls.

But Dr. Wienerkreis, I have a bad block here—I'd feel such a damned fool having an Edwardian rubber dog-bone about the house without having an Edwardian dog to chew it. Do you think I'd get over that? I'm afraid I might retreat into gross psychotic delusion—decide I was the only one who was sane, and start writing articles trying to make everyone else feel a damned fool for not feeling a damned fool.

Divine *News, Darlings!*

Among the aristocracy, reports a man at Glasgow University who has been studying their ways, one marriage in every four now ends in divorce. In other words, the aristocracy have reached the status of a Problem, and the Bishop of Twicester and I are deeply concerned about it.

"I am convinced," he writes in a helpful little booklet entitled *The Aristocracy Today: a Challenge and an Opportunity*, "that there is nothing fundamentally wrong with modern aristocrats. We hear a lot about the bad ones, but at heart most of them are perfectly decent and uncommonly high-spirited folk.

"The trouble is, they lack leadership. They have plenty of money to spend, and they're subjected to all sorts of unscrupulous commercial pressures. A regular barrage of suggestive advertising screams class, class, class at them seven days a week. Do we wonder they sometimes take the wrong turning?

"Those of us who go among them to any extent know how resentful they are of ill-informed criticism, and how lost and bewildered they feel in a world which seems to be run entirely for the benefit of their inferiors. My work takes me into a large club for lords and ladies in the parish of Westminster, and I know from personal experience how very likeable and human some of them can be. In a club like this, where they are given proper facilities for self-expression, there is very little hooliganism or other delinquency."

The Bishop and I believe that the Church isn't getting through to the aristocracy because it doesn't really speak their language. All this "thou" and "thee" and "yeah, yeah, yeah," mean nothing at all to the average lord. And many of the teachings of the Church—particularly those that lay stress on poverty and humility—seem to have little relevance to life as they know it.

We feel that the only reason so many lords hang about racecourses and grouse moors is that they have nowhere else to go. They drink and gamble and inflict suffering on animals because they're bored. We want to see more clubs set up for them along the lines of the one at Westminster. It doesn't take much—some red leather upholstery and a begged or borrowed woolsack—to turn the average church crypt into a very gay and inviting little House of Lords, where the local nobility can enjoy soft drinks together and take part in constructive activities such as debating.

These clubs should be places where lords and ladies can feel at home in the sort of clothes they like to wear—which may mean anything from baggy tweeds to the full traditional "gear" of robes and coronets! Sober citizens may sniff, but very smart some of them can look, believe me, when they're "dressed to kill" at the local meet!

Above all, we want to encourage the lords and ladies to do their divorcing in a healthy, open atmosphere of camaraderie and good fellowship, and get right away from the old hole-and-corner approach. Let all the questions and worries be thrashed out fully and frankly. "Can pre-marital divorce ever be right?" "Will I lose my husband if I refuse to divorce him?" You'll be amazed at the things that worry these high-spirited old families.

But this by itself is not enough—we must try to attract them into the churches. The Bishop made a remarkable start last Sunday by holding a Lord and Lady Day Service. He decorated the Cathedral with sporting prints, and replaced the choir and organist with Debrett Dansant and his Debs Delights, who rendered a number of hymns which the Bishop had translated into straightforward upper-class English, such as "Too super, too dishy, too marvellous Chap!"

His Lordship himself galloped in on horseback, wearing hunting pink and plus-fours. Crying "View halloo!" he threw a gun into his shoulder, gave the angels in the roof a right and a left, and brought down a cock and a hen. Pausing only to set the port circulating among the congregation, he got the Rural Dean to give him a leg up into the pulpit, where all the known tongues of dukes and of barons descended on him simultaneously, and he preached thus:

"My text today is from Ecclesiastes chapter 5 verse 12: 'The sleep of a labourin' man is sweet.' Or as we say, 'The sleep of a labourin' man is puddin'.'

"How true that is, what? I mean to say, sometimes we draw a covert for the meanin' of life, and it seems to double back and go to earth. I know I do, what? But when you go forth from here today I want you to bear in your hearts the knowledge that whenever things get too utterly ghastly, too absolutely filthington, you can always drop in on God for a quick spiritual snifter.

"You see, I like to think of prayer as a kind of spiritual grouse shootin'—a chance to get shot of the odd brace of grumbles. Yes, as I said in the Teenagers' Service last week, goin' out after the birds is as much a part of religion as toddlin' along to Vespers or Holy Communers. And doin' a ton in the Rolls is just about as religious as you can get short of actually goin' in for Holy Orders kit. I mean to say, what?

"To him who hearkeneth not to the voice of righteousness the consequences could be dashed desperate, not to say hellish. But the man who doth the best he can in the jolly old circs is likely to have a heavenly time, doncher know, what?

"Shall we Johann Sebastian kneelers-peelers?"

And the whole congregation—Mrs. Thrumley, Mrs. Arthur Upstreet, and the Lord Bishop's old mother—fell upon their knees and repented bitterly of the way of life that had brought them into that place.

A Question of Downbringing

My wife's studying sociology. She comes home from the lectures and teaches it to me over dinner, and one of the most interesting nuggets of sociological information I've been tossed across the cheese and biscuits so far is that my wife (a doctor's daughter) has married beneath her.

"It hadn't really struck me before," she said. "Journalists are lower-middle class."

"Don't talk tripe," I replied, with my usual scientific detachment.

"I'm not using the term with any emotive connotation," said my wife. "Its just a simple sociological fact. I had it from the lecturer less than an hour ago."

"Class is a matter of supreme indifference to me personally, as you know, so leave me out of it. But are you trying to tell me that people like the editor of the *Spectator* with his £40,000 house are lower-middle class? You take a look at the lads soaking up the hock in El Vino's and you won't go round screaming 'lower-middle class' like that."

"I'm not screaming anything. I'm giving you a piece of completely objective sociological information. Where do *you* think you come on the social scale, anyway?"

"Just about anywhere except the lower-middle class, if you really want to know. Working class, upper-middle class—I don't mind, just so long as it's not lower-middle."

"Because deep inside you know lower-middle's what you are. Everybody struggles to get off his own particular pin, and just succeeds in impaling himself harder and harder."

She showed me the tables—the Registrar-General's classification of social classes; the Hall-Jones scale; the A/B scale used by the Institute of Practitioners in Advertising. It was difficult to get round it, certainly. I'm clearly not a member of a learned profession (the top of everybody's list), or the daughter of one. I don't manage or administer anything. I'm not a skilled manual worker. The only possible hole for a man in my position seems to be Hall-Jones group 3 or 4 (Inspectional and Supervisory) or I.P.A. group C 1 (Supervisory and Clerical), on the grounds that I mind or supervise other people's business. And Group C 1 is clearly down in black and white as lower-middle class.

"Are you trying to tell me I'm worse than some crooked accountant or fly-by-night lawyer?" I shouted calmly.

"Who said anything about better or worse?" said my wife. "You're just lower down the social scale, that's all. There's no need to get upset about it."

"As if I'd get upset about some obsolete pseudo-concept like class!" I snarled, doing my best to be reasonable and conciliatory. "Look, I'm not trying to say I'm upper-middle class, or even middle-middle class. But as a matter of sober and objective self-assessment I do happen to believe that I'm *upper lower-middle*. Or at any rate upper-middle lower-middle."

"It's no good trying to persuade *me*," said my wife. "Take it up with the Registrar-General. Argue it out with the I.P.A. *I* can't change natural laws to suit your convenience."

"But don't you remember, before you started doing sociology, how we always used to feel tremendously middle-middle class together?"

"Michael, everyone thinks he's middle-middle class. It's just a romantic notion one has to grow out of. Let's face up to reality. You happen to be two or three social classes below me. That's all. I'm sure that with good will and understanding on both sides this needn't prove an insurmountable barrier."

It's a difficult subject all right, class. When Anthony Powell appeared on television, the *Radio Times* described him as a novelist who "satirises the upper-middle classes with a brilliant sense of social nuance."

The upper-middle classes? The Earl of Warminster, Sir Gavin Walpole-Wilson, General Conyers, Sir Magnus Donners-Brebner, Lady Ardglass, Lady Molly Jeavons, Prince Theodoric, and all the rest of those magnificent characters, *upper-middle* class?

Well, stap me! I thought they were the *upper* classes! I suppose that just shows my embarrassing lower-middle class naïvety. The *Radio Times*, with its brilliant sense of social nuance, saw immediately that all Powell's earls, courtiers, and great industrialists were really horribly bourgeois. And indeed, the whole upper class recedes like the horizon as you approach it. What could be more middle class than an earl or a courtier, when you come to think about it? Except perhaps a royal duke or an oil millionaire?

Indeed, as my wife pointed out when I raised the matter at my next tutorial, for sociological purposes the upper classes simply don't exist. The Registrar-General's classification and the Hall-Jones scale both start with the professional classes: the I.P.A. grading with group A, the upper-middle class.

"But, look," I protested, "the middle classes must be in the middle of something. They can't just be sandwiched between the lower classes and God."

"*Lower classes?*" said my wife. "What are they? You don't mean the working classes, do you?"

"What I'm getting at is, are you trying to tell me that you and your professional pals are higher up the social scale than earls and kings and so on?"

"It depends how the earls and kings spend their time, Michael. If they just inspect their troops and supervise the running of their estates I suppose they come in the Inspectional and Supervisory category along with you."

"What? You honestly think a doctor's daughter's higher up than a full-blown belted earl!"

"This is a surprisingly reactionary attitude you're taking up, Michael."

"Well, for heaven's sake! I mean, one does know certain things instinctively. I mean, well, for heaven's sake!"

No, let's be bold and radical. The upper classes have got to have somewhere to live, after all. I don't mind having them down here with me in the lower-middle classes. Just so long as they don't tell my smart friends they saw me down here, that's all I ask.

The Monolithic View of Mirrors

It is with a close and warmly sympathetic interest that all men of good will, whatever their creed, are following the vigorous debate now going on within the Carthaginian Monolithic Church on the vexed question of rear-view mirrors.

It has long been the teaching of the Church that looking backwards while travelling forwards is categorically and explicitly forbidden by God, since it was for doing this that He visited instant fossilisation upon Lot's wife.

In this context "looking back" has always been interpreted as frustrating the natural forward gaze of the traveller, whether by turning the head (*visus interruptus*), or by the interposition of a mechanical device such as a mirror.

Carthaginian Monolithic theologians claim that looking back is not only divinely prohibited, but can also be seen by the light of reason to be contrary to natural law, since it is patently interfering with nature to inhibit the inherent tendency of fast-moving objects to collide, and is frustrating the natural consequences of the act of driving.

Moreover, they argue, there is a strong aesthetic objection to looking back, since it must plainly detract from the spontaneity of the driving act, and they point out how much more insipid life becomes if the spice of the unexpected is removed altogether. It must in all fairness be pointed out that the keen interest of the Monolithic clergy in preserving spontaneity and avoiding insipidity is entirely altruistic, since they do not themselves drive.

These arguments notwithstanding, the Church has long recognised the need to prevent cars crashing into the back of one another indiscriminately, and Monolithics are permitted to avoid it by abstaining from driving altogether, or by driving only during the so-called "safe period," between midnight and six a.m., when the chances of being crashed into are greatly reduced.

Nevertheless, there is a sympathetic—indeed, anguished—realisation among many Monolithic leaders today that self-restraint alone may be inadequate to meet the situation. The question was less crucial in the days when the main effect of the doctrine was to prohibit Monolithics from sitting with their back to the engine in railway carriages. But the increasing popularity of the motor car is putting an intolerable burden upon the accident wards of the world's hospitals.

There is intense sympathy, too, for the great strain undergone by Monolithic drivers who have been run into from behind perhaps 13 or 14 times already, and who now scarcely dare drive home to see their wives if it involves turning right, or pulling out to pass a parked car.

It is to this agonising problem that "the box" may provide an answer. "The box" is a rearward radar scanning device which scientists are still testing. "Liberal" Monolithics believe that a scanning aerial cannot be said to "look" back in the natural sense of looking, and that the radar screen does not deflect the natural forward gaze of the driver, like a mirror, but is a natural part of his natural forward view.

It is emphasised that even if "the box" were to be accepted, it could never be used for merely selfish purposes, to avoid a crash simply because a crash was not desired, but only where a driver had already had three or four crashes, and there were genuine grounds for believing that another one might have a serious effect upon his health.

(o. j. sprout: *I must say, I'm greatly struck by the responsibility and fair-mindedness with which Mr. Frayn is treating this thorny subject.*

mrs. sprout: *I agree with you, Sprout. He's not a Carthaginian Monolithic himself, is he?*)

All the same, some authorities doubt if the box could ever be an acceptable compromise. They believe that the only hope would be to develop a device which would make the safe period principle more reliable—making absolutely sure that the road behind the car was kept clear by scattering perhaps nails or broken glass, perhaps small high explosive bombs.

(sprout: *You know, I don't think he's a Carthaginian Monolithic at all, Mrs. Sprout. That's the beauty of it. To me the whole article suggests the best traditions of agnostic liberal journalism.*)

Non-Monolithic observers can only look on at this debate with sympathy and understanding. They may be sure that it will be carried through with utter sincerity and a genuine sense of urgency, and that everyone on both sides will do his best, and play the game according to the rules.

(mrs. sprout: *There were tears in his eyes in the last paragraph, Sprout.*

sprout: *In mine too, Mrs. Sprout. I can only say that the whole inquiry was conducted with the beautiful reverence and respect which the subject demands.*)

Inside the Krankenhaus

I'm learning a lot from the series the *Daily Mirror* is publishing by Auberon Waugh and his wife ("the brilliant young Waughs," as the *Mirror* calls them). They're travelling about

Europe, sending back a piece a week on the national characteristics of each country they visit.

The Germans are the latest race to come under their microscope. "Our idea of the country," writes Mr. Waugh, "had been formed by seeing war films in which all Germans shout 'Ach so! Gott in Himmel!'" He was agreeably surprised to find that this was not the case in the Federal Republic today, and almost as surprised by the sheer variety of the German race. "Germans come in all sizes," he reports, "fat, thin, tall, short, dark, fair. Some are cheerful, some gloomy."

Ach so? one feels like gasping. Thin as well as fat? Short as well as tall? Some cheerful, some gloomy? Well, dash it all! Gott, as one might say, in Himmel!

So the old prejudices and misconceptions are at last exposed. There's only one thing in which Mr. Waugh thinks the Germans might be deficient, and that's a sense of the ridiculous—a grave flaw, of course, which sets them apart from visiting British journalists and others. Mr. Waugh thinks that their language might be in some way to blame.

"It must be very difficult to keep a straight face," he writes, "if, when you go to visit a relative in hospital you have to ask for the Krankenhaus, or when you want the way out, if you have to ask for the Ausfahrt."

I suppose it must. I'd never thought of it that way before. I suppose life must be just one long struggle to keep themselves from bursting out laughing at their own language.

It would explain a lot, of course. That's what the object of all that iron Prussian discipline must have been. That's what all those duelling scars were for—to camouflage the dirty grins on the faces of people inquiring about the Ausfahrt.

Now that the old traditional codes of discipline have gone it's terrible. The approach to every Ausfahrt, Einfahrt, and Krankenhaus in the Federal Republic is jammed with people falling about and holding their sides. But that's nothing to what it's like *inside* the Krankenhaus. Inside it sounds like 14 different studio audiences trying to earn their free tickets simultaneously, as the patients describe their various comic-sounding symptoms to the staff. Here's a new admission scarcely able to speak for giggles as he tells the doctor he has a pain in his elbow.

"A Schmerz in your Ellenbogen?" repeats the doctor without any sign of amusement—he's heard the joke before, of course. "Which Ellenbogen?"

"Both Ellenbogens," replies the patient, trying to pull himself together. "I also get agonising twinges which run up and down my leg from my ... from my...."

But it's no good—he's off again. Unable to get the words out for laughing, he points silently from his thigh to his ankle.

"From your Schenkel to your Knöchel?" says the doctor, the corner of his mouth twitching very slightly in spite of himself. The patient nods helplessly.

"And sometimes," he gasps, "and sometimes ... all the way down my...."

He closes his eyes and vibrates silently, shaking his head from time to time to indicate that speech is beyond him.

"Come on," says the doctor, frankly grinning himself now. "Get it out."

"All the way down my ... my Wirb ... my Wirbel...."

"You'll start me off if you're not careful. Your what?"

"My Wirbelsäu-häu-häu-häu-häu-häu-häu...."

"Your Wirbelsäule? Your backbone?"

The patient nods, his eyes covered with his hand, his shoulders shaking rhythmically. The doctor bites his lip hard to stop himself giving way.

"Any other symptoms?" he demands gruffly.

"Yes," croaks the patient weakly. "Verstopfung!"

At this the doctor can hold out no longer. A great snort of laughter forces its way past his clenched jaw muscles, and he puts his head back and laughs until he cries.

"Verstopft, are you?" he manages at last. "Constipated?"

"Verstopft up solid!"

Eventually they both simmer down a bit, and sigh, and wipe their eyes, smiling anywhere but at each other.

"You know what your trouble is?" says the doctor. "You've got Kniescheibenentzündung. Housemaid's knee."

"Don't!" pleads the patient. "You'll start me off again!"

"And a rather bad dose of...."

"No, honestly, I've got a pain as it is...."

"No, listen, a rather bad dose of Windpo-ho-ho-ho-ho-ho...!"

"Stop! Sto-ho-ho-ho-ho-ho...!"
"Wind ... Wind-hi-hi-hi-hi-hi...!"
"Oh ...! I swear I'm dying...!"
"Windpocken! Chickenpox!"
"No, honestly, shut up...!"
"*And....*"
"I'm not listening!"
"... You've sprained your—no, listen—your nostril, your Nasenflügel...!"

Well, the poor devil's in stitches already, of course. By the time he's had a splint applied to his Nasenflügel and been wheeled out towards the Ausfahrt, he's probably just about what German doctors call *blühendekopfabgelacht*—laughed his blooming head off. That's going to take a stitch or two to fix; it's yet another case of someone coming out of the Krankenhaus a whole lot kranker than he went in.

Gott in Himmel! It makes you glad to be English.

The Meteorological School

All afternoon the great fleets of slow-moving summer cumulus were coming up out of the south-west, solid and intricately moulded, touched in places with a hot coppery burnish, gravely pacing the immensity of the steppe. Sergei lay in the long grass and watched them, thinking about Anton Fyodorovich's house in Ryazan Province....

That's how one of my great unwritten novels starts. Another begins:—

The fog crept among the houses and patrolled the streets like the spies and pickets of an occupying army. All the sounds of the city were muted by its grey presence. Familiar landmarks loomed strange and menacing as one walked about, as if no old loyalty could be taken for granted under the new dispensation. Somewhere out in the great grey limbo in one of the open squares, Van der Velde caught the raw wetness of the air in his throat, and coughed. "Damn this fog," he said....

And another:—

> Just before noon a fine, warm, soaking rain began to fall, turning
> the dusty grey slates on the roof of the church a glossy black, and
> whispering monotonously in the topmost branches of the elms.
> The rain covered Mrs. Morton-Wise's spectacles with a film of fine
> droplets, making it increasingly difficult for her to see from where
> she stood what was happening on the other side of the church-
> yard. . . .

That's how they start, and that's how they stop. I'm all right
on the measured periods describing the weather. It's the entry
of Sergei, Van der Velde, Mrs. Morton-Wise, and the rest, that
puts the curse on them.

Who are all these people, anyway? I'm not sure that I'm
terribly interested. If Van der Velde's not fat he's thin, if he
hasn't got good digestion he's got bad digestion. All right, let's
say he's thin with bad digestion. He hates his father, say; he
marries a depressive heiress who deceives him with an art
dealer; he's accused of suppressing the truth about conditions
in a desiccated coconut factory. I don't know. Maybe he writes
a novel about a fat man with good digestion who runs off with
the wife of a schizoid bicycle designer. . . . So what? How can I
write fine prose about people's digestive troubles and bicycle
designers' wives?

The weather—that's what I want to write about. What
immensely evocative stuff weather is! Whenever I look out of
the window and observe the meteorological condition of the
day I can feel the grand periods pulsing in the blood, the
nostalgic phrases ringing in my head. Whenever I look at the
typewriter and see a blank piece of paper, the thin Atlantic
cloud-wrack starts to scud across it immediately.

I dare say I'm not the only one. Anyone with a liberal
education and a maritime climate probably feels the same.
English novelists on the whole keep the reader fairly continu-
ously informed about the temperature, humidity and wind
velocity in which their man reveals his inner nature and gets the
girl.

Most of my literary tastes were formed by the twin volumes
of prose passages for translation into and out of French which
we used in the sixth form at school—not surprisingly, since
translation is one of the few occasions on which one is obliged

to examine prose in close and intimate detail. I believe my addiction to meteorological romanticism is no exception. All the extracts seemed to be about nocturnal storms, the ending of great droughts, or summer nights spent out of doors in warm airs and brilliant starlight, and by the time one had looked it up in Mr. Mansion's invaluable French dictionary and decided whether the mist rising from the reed-beds as the dusk drew on was *brume, embrun, brouillard, brouillasse* or *brumasse*, the meteorological subtleties had made a considerable impression on one's subconscious.

One can of course revert to the weather pretty frequently during a novel (for instance, I can see that a day of gathering oppression, followed by a terrible nocturnal thunderstorm and a clear, sparkling morning, are going to take our minds off Sergei some time in the near future). But between whiles it's people, people, people. Before I can make a career for myself as a novelist (and is there any other honourable career for an arts graduate?), the people problem will have to be solved. Either I shall have to collaborate with someone who's good with people but lost when faced with the fine, steaming drizzle from the iron-grey overcast, or I shall have to found the meteorological school of novel writing.

It happened in painting. Once upon a time such weather and landscape as there was occurred only in portraits, fitted in very small between the subject's left ear and the frame. But the weather and the landscape expanded, and the heads shrank in the steadily increasing rainfall, until eventually the sun shone and the snow fell upon insignificant little fellows in the middle distance, or upon no one at all.

Now it's happening in the novel. Take what some critics consider the greatest of my unwritten works in this genre, "My Sun, My Sun." This is a ruthless and entirely uninhabited exposure of a high-pressure system centred over the Azores, which on a trip to Southern Ireland meets a weak trough of low pressure moving down from Iceland. Their encounter is tempestuous, and a cold front is born, which brings a routed cavalry of storm clouds trooping in from the sea, with scattered showers like torn banners streaming in the wind. . . .

And so on. It's one of the saddest things in the world that so much which is a pleasure to write is a pain in the neck to read.

Firm Friends of Ours

We've just had another of our regular visits from Christopher and Lavinia Crumble, our private consumer research, marriage guidance, home heating, and child welfare advisory service.

They come in about once a month and straighten us out. What I admire about them is their tremendous firmness in dealing with us. It's no good just offering vague suggestions to feckless problem families like us. You've got to tell us exactly what to do, and then you've to damn well stand over us and make sure we do it.

With their great sense of social responsibility and their unbounded moral energy, the Crumbles usually set to work even before they are through the front door.

"I see you've still got one of these old-fashioned locks," says Christopher. "You realise that any half-wit burglar could pick this with a bent pin and a nail-file in about five seconds flat? Couldn't he, darling?"

"Christopher will give you the address of the firm that imports those new draught-proof Swiss micro-precision locks," says Lavinia. "Won't you, darling?"

"Oh, I'll give their local office a ring tomorrow and get them to send you a fitter round right away. No, no—no trouble at all. Is it, darling?"

Christopher has scarcely had time to make a note in his diary before Lavinia has stepped back in amazement. Oh God, the doormat! We've forgotten about the doormat!

"You *said* you were going to get one of those hand-knitted Vietnamese ones like ours," says Lavinia. "Didn't they, darling? What happened? I mean, goodness knows, it's your home—it's up to you to decide what sort of doormat you want in it. But when it's been scientifically *proved* by independent experts that the hand-knitted ones have by far the highest mat-sole abrasion co-efficient. . .!"

By the time we sit down to dinner the Crumbles have already put our domestic economy right on a number of points, and it's the turn of my wife's cooking for a helping hand. But the tact they do it with!

"This apple-pie is absolutely marvellous, isn't it, darling?"

"Marvellous!"

"*Marvellous!* Of course, we've rather gone off having heavy pastry dishes on top of great, greasy meals—haven't we, darling?—and I've got a wonderful new recipe for mango sorbet that you absolutely *must* try."

"We think it's the *only* pudding in the world, don't we, darling?"

"Though, of course, we *adore* apple-pie, too."

It also turns out in the course of conversation—and this we had not known or suspected before—that we are absolutely obliged to read Ned Ogham's new novel (which Lavinia will send us) about a Midlands couple who keep a chicken grill, and who barbecue a passing encyclopaedia salesman in the Rotisso-mat as a sacrifice to the sun-god. We are under a further categorical imperative to see Fred Umble's new play (Christopher will get us the tickets) about a group of workers in an expanded polystyrene factory who ritually beat the tea-girl to death with plastic spoons, and eat her for lunch in a Dionysiac frenzy in the works canteen.

And what about the floor? Do we like it the way it is? inquires Christopher with all the old tact. Or shall he bring over the five-gallon drum of Simpson's "Florscraypa" they happen to have left from doing their lavatory, so we can really get down on our hands and knees this weekend and start all over again?

"Of course," says Lavinia, "it would make all the difference to the room if the *ceiling* were brightened up a bit, wouldn't it, darling?"

"They'd be far better off with *something* on the ceiling, certainly. How about *wallpaper!*"

"*Yes!* One of those rather William Morrissy ones!"

"That's a tremendously exciting idea, darling. We'll pop along to that little man of ours in Muswell Hill tomorrow and see what he's got."

"Then we could throw out that ghastly old sofa and get a chaise-longue. We could cover it with one of those rather art-nouveauish prints, couldn't we, darling?"

They're also going to get our children into a marvellous pre-nursery school that all our friends use, with a very high pass rate into the top nursery schools in the district, though whether to send them now or after the Christmas exam season they haven't quite decided yet. They don't think there's any need to worry too much about the children's development, we're relieved to hear, provided we treat them as rational human beings, on a man-to-man basis, the way the Crumbles would treat their own children, if they had any.

"Of course, what children need most," explains Lavinia, "as psychiatrists now agree, is a constructively disturbed home background."

"As I expect you know," smiles Christopher, "the really well-adjusted couples aren't the ones who are so suspiciously polite and loving to one another all the time. Are they, darling?"

"No—the really well-adjusted couples are the ones who fight like cat and dog at every opportunity. We have the most tremendously helpful fights, don't we, darling?"

"Oh, all the time. We were just thinking the other day— weren't we, darling?—that whenever we see you two you scarcely so much as say a word to each other. It's very bad to bottle it all up, you know. If you want to have a bit of a scrap, you go ahead. We don't mind. Do we, darling?"

Heavens, we're grateful for all they've done for us. About the only service left unperformed is to tell us that of course our breath smells *marvellous*, but we absolutely *must* try a wonderful little deodorant toothpaste they know about....

How about it, darlings?

Substance Without Soul

It's curious how plastics are so universally disliked as materials. Or perhaps not so much disliked as despised, as if they were in some way *morally* inferior. Everyone uses them, and everyone despises them, just as the rich use and despise the poor.

Not *you*, of course, open-minded reader. I know you've got an entirely sensible attitude towards plastics, as towards everything else. But take me. In our house we eat off china plates, which break if you drop them. We drink out of glasses, which break if you look at them. We have plaster walls and wooden furniture, neither of which are capable of surviving the proximity of normally active human beings. How is it in your house, open-minded reader?

Most people's first objection to plastics, I think, would be that they frequently try to ape their betters and pass themselves off as other materials. But they disguise themselves only to avoid our contempt for plastics as plastics, and to plastics as plastics I think our principal moral objections are these:—

They don't feel right. They're too cold to the touch, or too warm; too smooth, or too tacky. To put it bluntly, they don't feel like leather or stone or wood or metal. They feel like, well, like plastics.

They're unnatural. That is, they're not got by hewing, mining, quarrying, smelting, tanning, or any of the other robust age-old processes by which we get proper materials. I say "we." I don't mean "we" in the sense of "you and I," of course—I don't suppose you or I have ever done much quarrying or smelting. I mean "we" in the sense of "someone."

They're too bland. They have no grain or quirkiness—no innate character which imposes itself upon us. Like a subject race they are too obedient to be respected.

Thus, they can be worked too easily. I don't mean that you or I could work them. Of course we couldn't—we haven't got the right tools, and we couldn't tell a polyester from a polyanthus, anyway. I mean that you don't have to roll up your sleeves and forge plastics, or carve them, or otherwise bend them to your will by sheer physical skill, as you do with proper materials. Or as someone does.

Dammit, they're not produced by individual craftsmen at all. They're turned out by faceless industrial organisations equipped with immensely expensive plant, and staffed by ordinary faceless functionaries like you and me.

Anyway, they're too cheap. They're cheaper than the materials for which they're alternatives, which is damning enough in itself; and because they're cheaper, goods made in plastics are usually more widely distributed, to poorer people with commoner tastes.

I'm not sure that this last objection isn't the strongest of the lot. After all, china-clay is bland and easily-worked. Glass is cold and unnatural. Stainless steel and diamonds are produced by immense corporations equipped with remote-controlled electric furnaces.

Still, I dare say we shall come round to the new material eventually. We usually do. I seem to remember that when I was a child the word "cotton" had a rather deprecating ring. It went with "thin" and "flimsy," as in descriptions of under-nourished girls wearing cheap make-up and shivering in their thin cotton dresses. Cotton was the poor man's substitute for wool or silk. Then they invented nylon and the rest; and now a genuine cotton shirt is the luxurious alternative to a hard-wearing, drip-dry, artificial one.

Thatch was once endured by the poor, and is now restored by the rich. Fur-coats were no doubt regarded much like denim overalls until someone invented weaving, and hunting declined. Denim, indeed, has risen from overalls to ladies' play-suits. Even poor old chromium plate begins to be treated with respect, now that we can look back with nostalgia from the thin chromium-plating put on cars today to the thick, rich, incorruptible stuff they trowelled on before the war.

One can imagine with what disdain the last of the Neolithics looked upon the incoming tide of flash, cheap bronzewear; and how young married Bronze Agers kept bronze cutlery for the children, and proper flint knives, which broke if you dropped them, for their guests. And how the first grasping entre-preneurs of the Iron Age made their money selling character-less iron teaspoons in Woolworths, and spent it on buying for their own use fine antique bronze teaspoons rescued by astute dealers from the nurseries of an earlier generation.

Not all materials make the grade—corrugated iron hasn't for one. But I confidently expect before I die to be buying back at reassuringly high prices the plastic junk I'm throwing out now, and hanging it reverently around the antique plastic panelling. I see myself at some great age settling back in my cosy old P.V.C.-covered swivel chair and watching a learned team on television discussing the lost glories of the Age of Plastic.

"This delightful little figurine of a cowboy," some expert will be saying, turning it over lovingly in his fingers "dates from the early 1960s, and was probably given away with a breakfast food, so general was pride in art and fine craftsmanship then.

"This sort of work was being done in literally hundreds of small workshops up and down the country. It's difficult for us today, I think, to realise what a tremendous atmosphere of creative excitement there must have been in the air at that time. The whole nation must have seemed to be bursting forth into plastic song. Why, the very names of the materials those old craftsmen used are a hymn of praise in themselves— polystyrene, polyethylene, polypropylene, polymer resin, polyurethane, polyolefines; cresylics and phenolics; acrylonitrile-butadiene-styrene...."

Not like the ghastly range of materials they'll be using by then. Unnaturally resistant to all forms of damage, with some ludicrous form of grain or texture to boot.

And *outrageously* cheap.

Business Worries

Children and animals are always reckoned to be the great scene-stealers against whom actors are reluctant to compete. But to my mind the greatest scene-stealer of all in films is a corpse.

Whatever the other attractions on the screen, if there's a corpse about I gaze at it fixedly. I have a nagging ambition to catch the actor who plays the corpse breathing when he thinks everyone's forgotten about him. A small ambition for a grown man, I dare say, but it gives me a hobby.

No luck so far, though I may have blinked just at the crucial moment. I suppose those bodies *are* actors holding their breath? It's not all faked up somehow with corpses rented out from the mortuary and just made up to look like actors holding their breath? I must write in and ask the fan magazines.

Anyway, it shows you how relaxed and secure one can be in the cinema, knowing nothing can really go wrong except the projector or the air-conditioning. It's a very different matter in the theatre. One wouldn't dare so much as glance at a corpse on the stage. After that great sword-fight all the way up the set and back one knows the poor man's bosom must be heaving up and down like a piledriver. One wouldn't dream of embarrassing him by looking. Anyway, he might feel one's eye on him and start to cough. No doubt, for that matter, he's fallen with one leg agonisingly doubled up—on his keys—with his ruff tickling his nose. His whole situation doesn't really bear thinking about too much.

All the time in the theatre one is waiting aghast for some embarrassing disaster to occur. Whenever there's a pause, one starts praying they're not going to forget their lines, or be taken ill on the stage. It's like walking through a minefield. Every day in the papers one reads about actors having heart attacks in the middle of their performance, breaking their legs, getting their heads split open in the fights, knocking themselves out against the scenery, and generally making a spectacle of themselves. At any moment, one feels, there might be some sort of scene.

Audience anxiety reaches a peak, as all sado-masochistic producers know, whenever the cast indulge in one of those little bits of business which depend on physical dexterity, or the workings of some notoriously fallible machine. My heart leaps into my mouth every time somebody offers to light somebody else's cigarette with a lighter. Flick—it fails to light! Flick—and again it doesn't light! Flick—look intently at ceiling, think about something else.

Flick—there's no logical reason why we shouldn't be stuck here all night, not daring to breathe, while he grinds away at the thing. Flick—will he give up after 10 flameless flicks? After a hundred? Flick—or does the action absolutely depend on this girl's having a drag? Flick—praise heaven, there's a flame!

But *now* they're both shaking so much that they can't get the flame and the cigarette to meet! Yes! No! Yes—they've done it! "Ah, that's better," she sighs contentedly, blowing out a thoughtful column of smoke. But, crumbling sanity, there *is* no smoke! The cigarette's gone out again!

One's palms sweat. Of course, one keeps telling oneself that it doesn't really matter, because no one nowadays expects a naïvely literal realism in the theatre. One wants to see the figures on the stage both as the actors acting and the characters acted. In a sense, of course, one's consciousness of this valuable duality is if anything heightened when one or two little things go slightly. . . .

Oh God, he's not going to throw her the revolver! Of course, they rehearse these things for weeks. . . . She's dropped it. Now she's picked it up—she's carrying bravely on. Don't feel you need to be brave on my account, dear. Honestly, it didn't embarrass me a bit. No, I had my eyes shut. I mean, I know I caught my breath when he threw it, but. . . . I suppose you can't possibly have *heard* me catching my breath, can you? I mean, it wasn't my catching my breath that made you . . . ? Oh, *God*!

I have a haunting fear that one night when I'm present some piece of business is going to go so completely wrong that the play as written cannot proceed at all, and the actors will be reduced to improvising some new line of development entirely. Take the famous Locket scene at the end of "Error for Error," when young Ferdinand shows Duke Oregano and the assembled court the locket which proves he is the Duke's son, carried off at birth by a waterspout. Suppose that after the lines—

A locket sav'd I from that spoutsome day,
Most curiously inscrib'd. I have it here.

Ferdinand tosses the vital instrument to the Duke, and the Duke fumbles it and drops it out of sight. What can they do, except make the rest of the scene up as they go along?

DUKE: Alas! Methinks I have misfinger'd it!
FERDINAND: Sire, bend thou down thine aged frame
And do thou smartly pluck it up again.
DUKE: Bend as I might, I cannot see the thing.
My lords, do you explore your cloggy beards.
No sign? Ah me, I fear it must have roll'd
Amid this mazy grove of cardboard trees.
FERDINAND: Was not one glance as it came winging by
Enough to grasp the general sense of it?
—That here before thee stands thy long-lost son?

DUKE: A fig for *your* problems—what worrieth me
  Is how I speak my major speech, which starts:
  "Come, locket, let me kiss thee for thy pains,
  And taste the savour of fidelity,"
  Without the bloody locket. Come, let's shift
  This forest. Take the yonder end and heave.
FERDINAND: Is this meet welcome for a long-lost son?
DUKE: Meet welcome for a long-lost son, forsooth!
  What kind of long-lost son is this, that chucks
  Essential props outside my senile reach,
  And cuts his long-lost father's longest speech?
  Lose thee again, son, till thou learnst at last
  The art of throwing props and not the cast.

Childholders

What my wife and I have now got more of than anything else, it occurred to me the other day, as I staggered through the front door with another armful of the stuff, is child-handling equipment.

I mean devices for holding small children up, holding them down, moving them along, and keeping them in one place. We must have got a hundredweight of the stuff. The only thing we're a bit short of is the children for all this wealth of plastic and bent tinplate to be used upon. I keep counting up incredulously, and we've only got two.

We're thinking of opening our home and making the collection public. I've been compiling a catalogue. What I've tried to do is to provide the visitor—and indeed myself—with some sort of *catalogue raisonné*; a coherent, step-by-step account of exactly how we came to build our great collection up.

The first exhibit is

I THE PRAM. Naturally there must be a pram. All children have prams. Where we were rather shrewd, I think, was in choosing a special patent collapsible model which at the turn of a nut lifts off the wheels to become a cot, or subsides into a push-chair. In which case, why do we need

2 THE CARRY-COT? Well, you see, the patent collapsible pram's downstairs and the bedroom's upstairs. And in any case, without the wheels the top of the patent collapsible pram would have to stand among the draughts on the floor. Whereas the carry-cot can stand on

3 THE CARRY-COT STAND. A great economy, a carry-cot and stand, because we didn't need a crib. All we needed was

4 THE DROP-SIDE COT. Now why the devil did we need a drop-side cot when we had a carry-cot? Because the baby had grown too big for the carry-cot. Then why didn't we skip the carry-cot and get a drop-side cot in the first place? Well, have you ever walked through the streets carrying a baby in a drop-side cot?

5 THE FOLDING WEEKEND BED. Why, you ask patiently, didn't we take the drop-side cot away for weekends? Because we'd have needed a larger car. A folding weekend bed was cheaper than a larger car.

All right so far? Now,

6 THE PUSH-CHAIR. We must have forgotten, you laugh, about that patent collapsible pram we started with which turned into a push-chair at the turn of a nut, the wrench of a bolt, the heave of the chassis, and the couple of thumps with the starting-handle. By no means. The fact is, the patent collapsible pram is now occupied by the second baby, while the original infant sits on top in

7 THE CLAMP-ON SEAT FOR ELDER CHILD. What?— you scream—why isn't the elder child sitting in the brand-new push-chair? Now, come, come. My wife could scarcely walk to the shops pushing the pram *and* the push-chair. Good God, man, you cry, make the elder child *walk*! Certainly. But this the elder child would consent to do only if bought

8 THE TOY PUSH-CHAIR to push. Unfortunately, the toy push-chair turned out to be large enough for the elder child to sit in and wait to *be* pushed. So we had to get her

9 THE DOLL'S PRAM, of a type so small that there was no room for the elder child. Indeed, there was only just enough room for the elder child to cram the younger child in. So the younger child had to be placed in protective custody inside

10 THE PLAY-PEN, from which it was released only to be sat up for meals in

11 THE PATENT ADJUSTABLE ALL-PURPOSE BABY CHAIR. Now why on earth couldn't we sit the child up in the clamp-on pram seat? Because the only thing the clamp-on pram seat clamped on was the pram, and the pram was downstairs. The patent adjustable all-purpose baby chair, however—strongly recommended by a liberal-radical woman's page—proved to have one small drawback; it turned upside-down if the child moved. The child did move. The answer, we felt, was not a high chair, but—much more economical—

12 THE CAR-SEAT, because it could be used both in the car and on the back of an ordinary chair at table. Then

13 ANOTHER CAR-SEAT, because the baby could lever the first one right off the chair. Then

14 THE HIGH CHAIR, because the baby could lever the second car-seat right off the chair, too. Then

15 THE SMALL CHAIR for the elder child, to stop it jealously insisting on sitting in the younger child's high chair.

16 THE CARRYING SLING, for taking younger child on health-giving nature rambles (don't tell me we should have pushed the patent collapsible pram over all those stiles and up all those mountains). Unfortunately the sling—strongly recommended by the liberal-radical woman's page—exerted intolerable pressure on the top of my spinal cord, and the agony was relieved only by the child falling out. Replaced by

17 THE RUCKSACK SEAT, a rugged structure of solid welded steel, recommended by the same damned liberal-radical woman's page. We hadn't got very far up the first mountain when it struck me that steel and child together, presumably, had the same effect on the heart as being three stone over-

weight. Came down the mountain hastily, and haven't tested the equipment since.

That's as far as the collection goes at present. Just the 17 items. No doubt we shall add to it in time.

The only other point of interest, I think, is that between them (if I have counted correctly) the 17 exhibits are decorated with 43 frogs, 47 rabbits, 51 fairies, 108 pussy-cats (60 with bows), 46 pigs, 96 ducks, 48 dwarfs, 103 mice, 204 doggies (40 of them stark naked), and one rat.

And I may say that every one of them, except the rat, is grinning fit to bust.

My Nature Diary

JANUARY: Out and about, as usual, striding across the local public recreation ground, observing Nature and the slow turning of the seasons. Brace of children gambolling and snapping at heel, ready for anything, particularly a sudden encounter with a bag of sweets or a television programme. Can't help noticing the grass—blade after blade of it, with a fine display of common brown mud (*terra fusca vulgaris*) coming through.

How one longs for February, the *real* fag-end month of winter, with its raw, murky, desolate afternoons expiring in sodden fields! Plan richly gloomy afternoon trips throughout February to the Fens and the dank industrial landscapes of the Thames Estuary.

FEBRUARY: Out and about on the public recreation ground. Grass still doing well. Children put up an old cock Smarties packet, its brilliant colouring showing up vividly against the mud. Order them to put it down again.

Weather oddly unsuitable for fens or marshes. Sudden warm, bright days occur, making one unable to think of anything except those sudden warm, bright days which will occur in March and touch one's heart with the first advance publicity for spring. Swear that for once I will be ready to make the most of them by dashing out to Kentish oast-houses surrounded by blossom, to the crocuses on King's Backs.

MARCH: Neat green and brown of native recreation ground spoiled by disgusting litter of old almond blossom. These blossom-louts should be prosecuted.

Too busy thinking about April to go anywhere. Ah, April! When the first brilliant greenery softens the gnarled timber of this ancient winter world! And we shall see it happen along the Quai d'Anjou and in the gardens of the Hotel Biron. Because in April we shall be in Paris! Or in Amsterdam. Or possibly in Venice, still fresh and cool and sparkling!

APRIL: I mean, of course, that we shall be there in May. Always expect the spring to happen in April, and realise only when April arrives that it happens in May. Meanwhile, observe the immutable march of Nature's timetable on the recreation ground, as the local dogs are brought out each day to move their bowels.

MAY: May somehow goes by before I have time to notice what Nature's doing on the recreation ground, let alone get tickets to fail to notice it elsewhere. *June*'s the month, of course. Midsummer; full leaf; the fresh prime of the year. To hell with the tawdry pleasures of foreign cities—in June I will take a knapsack and a stout stick and stride through the heartlands of England. Through Warwickshire, Worcestershire, Gloucestershire, Oxfordshire; through old towns full of bells and strong ale; through ancient green forests where temporarily dispossessed dukes wander with their courts, hunting the deer and communing in blank verse as fresh as spring-water.

JUNE: Take up my stout umbrella and stride through the heartlands of the recreation ground, now gaily bedecked with the Lesser and Greater Paper Bag, the Common Orangeskin, and the shyly peeping Lolly Stick.

How half-hearted, wishy-washy June makes one long for the great heats of July! They'll find me and my family in the simmering uplands of the Aveyron—no, in the sweltering, dusty plains of Emilia—no, no, in the burnt brown hills of Umbria! Solid iron heat will enclose us! Pulsating, suffocating heat! Ah!

JULY: While waiting for the great heats to arrive, walk about the recreation ground with my old 12-bore umbrella in the crook of my arm, unable to see anything but a vision of August. August is water, of course. Sunlit blue water, creaming surf. Have now saved such an enormous amount of money by not going to Paris or Amsterdam or Emilia or Umbria, and not buying a stout stick, that we could surely afford to spend August in Cyrenaica, or on the wild coast of Maine.

AUGUST: Funny—we couldn't. Spend August at home, thinking about September. My God, in September we'll go *anywhere*.

SEPTEMBER: And, indeed, in the ghastly little resort of N'Importe-Où we end up. Exercise our children by walking them on the local *terrain de récréation*. The yellowing leaves are being brought down by the rains and the equinoctial gales. Makes one deeply nostalgic for the golden-red autumn melancholy of England in October.

OCTOBER: Observe, on my rambles across the home recreation ground, that grass and mud do not in fact turn golden-red in autumn. The month we're all waiting for is November, when London really comes into its own, and the afternoon sun goes down blood-red into the foggy mercantile exhalations of the city. You'll find me in November mooning among the cranes and warehouses of Bankside, and calling at tea-and-crumpet time on friends with houses in Queen's Gate and Onslow Square and the Boltons, as the nannies dawdle home from the smoky Park with children in leggings.

NOVEMBER: I remember now—I haven't got any friends in Queen's Gate, Onslow Square, or the Boltons. Well, to hell with South Kensington and November. My own rude native recreation ground will look incomparably beautiful when December comes, and the green grass and brown mud disappear beneath that first soft snowfall of winter.

DECEMBER: Get out and about on the recreation ground, children at heel, yapping after ice-creams. Make a rain-man for them and organise a rainball fight. How one longs for January and February, the *real* winter months, when one starts to feel the first intimations of spring—spring, with all its sweet anticipation of a summer pregnant with winter-heralding autumn. . . . !

Lives and Likenesses

Mr. Ken Russell seems to have hit upon a simple but important new biographical principle in his films for "Monitor" on B.B.C. Television. According to sympathetic critics, he makes each film in the style of the artist it is about.

Thus, according to Peter Black, "his Elgar was straight-forward and sentimentalised, his Debussy misty and complex." His Douanier Rousseau, similarly, was naïve and primitive. In fact it was considerably *more* naïve and primitive than Rousseau. It takes a real hardened professional to get as naïve and primitive as that. These amateur innocents like Rousseau never knew the tricks of the trade.

Writers have obviously been missing an opportunity. In fact, it's rather presumptuous, when you come to think about it, for old Strachey to have written "Queen Victoria" in his own style and not Queen Victoria's. And why didn't Mr. Alan Bullock couch his study of Hitler rather more in the familiar Nuremberg vein? A touch of egomania here?

Now Mr. Russell has shown the way, no doubt the idea will be taken up. Here are trailers for one or two biographies I hope to be seeing in the book-shops soon.

Firstly I should like to say this—and I make no apology for mentioning it: Harold Wilson was born—and I choose that word advisedly—on the eleventh of March 1916. Not on the tenth, or the twelfth, as some people would like you to believe—and here I intend no disrespect to the many men and women up and down the country who I know *were* born on the tenth or the twelfth, and who have given loyal and unstinting service to the community, and whose special needs—I say this to them now—have not been forgotten.

But—and it's a big but—if this book is to make any real headway, if we're really going to bring it up to date, we simply cannot afford—and this cannot be said too often—we simply cannot afford to sit back and rest content with our progress so far. Because make no mistake—and there's none of us who doesn't make mistakes at times—if we're forced to go on breaking off like this for modifications, concessions, and re-assuring asides, we shan't reach Mr. Wilson's first birthday until about Chapter 23.

A (indef. art.) man who might with some justice be called the
AARDVARK (noun) of English letters, whose
AARONIC (adj.) pronouncements upon anything from the
AASVOGEL (noun) to the
ABACA (noun) often took his companions
ABACK (adv.), and frequently caused them to
ABANDON (verb) themselves to mirth, Dr. Johnson was never known to let anyone
ABASE (verb) or
ABASH (verb) him, and would wallow agreeably
ABASK (adv.) in what others might have found to be a veritable conversational
ABATTOIR (noun).

Mozart:
Chapter No. 21 in D Minor

In 1779 Mozart returned to Salzburg. In the year 1779 Mozart returned to Salzburg. Back to his native city in the year after 1778 Wolfgang Amadeus Mozart came.

And was made court organist, was appointed organist at the court, the organ-player at the court he was created. Having come back to Salzburg in 1779 he became court organist, the court organist is what he became after his return to Salzburg in 1779.

He was oppressed with debts. He owed money. Goods and services had been credited to him for which he had not yet paid. He was oppressed with debts, debts weighed him down. Money was outstanding. He owed. Money was what he owed.

In 1779 Mozart returned to Salzburg. Back to his home town came he. And was appointed court organist.

To Salzburg, the well-known town in Austria. That was where, in 1779, Mozart returned.

A Life of T. S. Eliot:
Acknowledgments

How can I begin to thank
Professor Pomattox, or Doctor Frack,
The Misses Fischbein, or Monsignor Blum?
Words lose their meaning, and grow slack.

Some typed upon Remingtons in obscure rooms.
Some made suggestions.
Some read the proofs. Some wept. One smiled:
"The world is full of questions."

Mrs. Crupper came and went
With tiny jars of liniment.

The finished pages flutter to the floor.
La lune éternue et s'endort.
All this, and so much more,
And so much more.

School of Applied Art

There's a lady in Kensington, according to the papers, called Mrs. Thorne, who runs conversation classes "for the sophisticate who finds small talk difficult." In seven hours, at 10 guineas the course, she teaches her case-load of sophisticates to get round their incapacity by talking about art.

We sophisticates have long known about the old art dodge, of course. The trouble has been up to now (if my own case is typical) that while we find small talk difficult, we don't get on too well with the big stuff, either. This has cost some of us dear in lost opportunities for business and romance.

Mrs. Thorne has hit upon two great complementary principles which make big topics accessible to small talkers. "It's just a question of learning what to say," she insists; and, "It doesn't matter what people say as long as they say something."

Armed before and behind with these two weapons of war, the sophisticate advances into any social gathering and merely looks round the room until his eye falls upon a picture. If it happens to be a Constable, Mrs. Thorne advises that you should mention you have just come back from the Constable country. If it's a Van Gogh, she suggests greeting it with a remark like "I always wonder what sort of painting he'd have done if he'd been entirely sane." (If you want to know what to say if it happens to be a Vermeer or a Leonardo, or a Guardi or a Braque, take your 10 guineas along and ask Mrs. Thorne.)

Anyway, it's clear that Mrs. Thorne is providing in seven hours what at the universities it still takes three solid years to acquire—a thorough practical grounding in the humanities, of the sort which years of experience have shown to fit graduates for a career in industry or government, for the management of scientists, and for the selection of a wife or husband.

Take the case of Harley Sparrowdew, bachelor and sophisticate. In the documentary film I am preparing on the Thorne system for Unesco, we see him at a brilliant gathering of industrialists, playwrights and Cabinet Ministers, a vodkatini in one beautifully manicured hand, gazing profoundly at a rather unsophisticated painting of a yellow chair. Suddenly he becomes aware that the lovely sophisticate Soignée Cheroot is standing silently beside him, lost in contemplation of the picture, too.

"What I always wonder," breathes Soignée raptly, "is what sort of painting he'd have done if he'd been entirely sane."

Sparrowdew turns and gazes at her. For a moment the world seems to stand still.

"You wonder that?" he asks softly. "Because so do I. Always. Night and day I ask myself, 'What kind of thing would this man have done if he'd been normal?'"

"I know. I know. The question haunts one. Oh *God*, I know the feeling!"

"It seems to me that if he could just have got away from this terrible sick obsession with chairs, he might—who knows?—have painted something quite normal. A table—a sideboard."

"Yes! Or a hatstand, or a cocktail-cabinet. Something clean and wholesome! Something that says yes to life!"

"Yes! That's it *exactly*...."

A century later—or is it only 10 minutes?—they have slipped away from the vacuous social throng, and are sitting at a sidewalk café beneath the stars. Somewhere, soft music is playing.

"I realised you were an Old Thornian, too, from the first moment," Sparrowdew is saying, gazing into her eyes. "I felt at once that we had the same background, that we were interested in the same things. I felt—oh, I don't know—we spoke each other's language. When you said that wonderful thing about Van Gogh—'I always wonder,' you said (I shall never forget it), 'what sort of painting he would have done if he had been entirely sane'—when you said that I felt somehow it was all preordained. I felt as if our whole thing was written down somewhere in some great book. You know what I mean?"

"Yes! I feel that if I hadn't said it first you would have said it yourself."

"I feel that, too. It's your tenderness, your deep *concern* for Van Gogh, that moves me."

"Our education taught us both to ask questions."

"To wonder. To have a sense of wonder."

"Yes! And the tremendous freedom with which one learnt to speak!"

"The feeling that it didn't matter what one said—all that mattered was the act of saying, the act of being articulate!"

They sit in silence for some minutes, absorbed in the thoughts they have conjured up.

"It was terrible when one first came down from Mrs. Thorne's," says Sparrowdew slowly. "One's first contact with the real world outside. It seemed so—so bleak and grimy. One went from party to party, and nowhere did one see a Constable or a Van Gogh on the wall. One's education seemed wasted, irrelevant."

"I felt exactly the same. Exactly!"

"The odd Piper lithograph, perhaps, the occasional Colquhoun sketch. The phrases one had learnt sounded hollow in one's mouth."

"But gradually...."

"Gradually it began to make sense. People listened. Personnel officers—managing directors. Older and wiser heads than one's own saw the advantage of having a man with a sense of curiosity about Van Gogh in charge of research."

"Or on the Board."

"Slowly everything fell into place. One perhaps bought one's Constable or one's Van Gogh. Bit by bit, with maturity, the point of it all became clear. All one lacked was someone who understood to share it with."

"Until tonight...."

"Until tonight.... Did I tell you I'd just come back from the Constable country, incidentally? I've got one or two slides I took of it, if it's not too late to come back to my place and have a look at them...."

The Normal Fifth

The normal home contains a pet, and the normal pet is a cat or a budgerigar, according to the statistics in the Official Handbook published by the Central Office of Information. The normal man, it appears, spends the normal evening at home with his cat or his budgerigar in front of his television set.

The leader-writer in the *Daily Mail* is appalled by the picture the figures conjure up. "What a miserable collection of stick-in-the-muds we are!" he writes. "Why don't we go out and enjoy ourselves? Why don't we throng the streets, talk to our neighbours, or sit about in cafés just looking at people?"

Sit about in cafés just looking at people? Sit about in which cafés, just looking at what people? In the Nell Gwynne Tea Shoppe in the High Street? Looking at old Mrs. Poorly and her friend Ida Know eating buttered scones?

And throng which streets, pray? Throng Delamere Gardens, N.W.12? Throng Jubilee Road, Screwe? There are some streets which in my experience are really pretty well unthrongable.

117

Anyway, whatever the pleasures of street-thronging, it's "splendidly normal people" that the National Children Adoption Association are looking out for to become adoptive parents, according to the secretary in *The Times*. What seems splendidly normal to the N.C.A.A. turns out to be remarkably similar to what seems normal to the Central Office of Information, except that the N.C.A.A.'s standards of normality are so searching that only one in five of their applicants turns out to be splendidly normal enough to qualify.

The ideal couple, says the secretary, probably live in the outer suburbs, and have a middle-sized detached or semi-detached house with a garden. "They are splendidly normal people, in good health and completely without neuroses now or in the past. He probably goes up to the City every day and she has no ambitions outside her home and her family. They usually have a pet—a cat or a budgerigar, and they don't have a lot of outside interests. But this doesn't mean to say they need to be exactly dull."

Of course, when one hears about all the splendidly normal people like this, one cannot help worrying once again about the abnormal ones, and what can be done to help them. Because, let's face it, there *are* abnormal people around; we can't just shrug the problem off and pretend they don't exist.

Some of them have only mild abnormalities, such as living in large houses, or keeping dogs, which might disqualify them from adopting children, but which need not otherwise prevent them leading decent and useful lives.

But a few of them do suffer from gross abnormalities, like not working in the City. Progel, in "The Abnormal Englishman," identifies this condition as dysmetropolia, and attributes it to the absence or inadequacy of the patient's uncle-figures during adolescence. He sees working in other parts of the country as a subconscious evasion of reality—a symptom of neurosis allied to, and often co-present with, neurotic manifestations such as dropping aitches, doing manual work and playing out masochistic guilt-fantasies by refusing to earn a normal middle-sized salary.

Hergstrom takes a more radical view. He believes that everyone, however disturbed, *knows* somewhere inside him that he works in the City and lives in a middle-sized suburban house with a budgerigar, and that delusions to the contrary are merely hysterical.

McStride and Leastways, in their classic study "Behaviour Patterns of Budgerigarlessness," put more emphasis on learned reflexes. One of their most grossly disturbed patients presented an extraordinary range of symptoms. He lived in a *terraced house* in *Sheffield*, worked in a *factory*, and confessed that he often *went out in the evening*.

McStride and Leastways achieved a partial cure by attaching electrodes to the patient, and administering painful electric shocks when he went to work, when he came home, and when he went out again at night. After prolonged treatment the patient moved to Nottingham, which was at any rate 37 miles along the road to recovery from his dysmetropolia. (When last heard of he was undergoing further conditioning therapy to overcome his irrational dread of electricity.)

The abnormality symptoms presented by women can sometimes be even more serious. In his survey of married women arrested for reading in Beckenham Public Library, Didbold estimates that there may be as many as 200 or even 300 married women in this country suffering from ambitions outside the home and family.

According to Meany, outside ambitions in women are the result of emotional deprivation in infancy, possibly aggravated by over-intense educational experience. He wants the Government to launch a crash programme for the early detection of unnatural ambition, and warns that if nothing is done the country may in a year or two's time face a full-scale epidemic.

In both men and women, ambitions and interests outside the home tend to be the most dangerous abnormalities, if allowed to go unchecked. Strabolgi, for instance, has demonstrated a definite correlation between extra-domiciliary interests and certain forms of criminal behaviour. In his sample of 317 men and women in the Barnet area, *not one* committed burglary, simony, or robbery with violence while sitting at home watching the television.

It's true that 14 were later convicted of tax offences, six of wounding their wives, and one of strangling his budgerigar.

But that's normal.

The Battle of the Books

The literary quiz game on BBC2 "Take It or Leave It," is driving me into the depressives' ward.

They read extracts from well-known books to a panel of four, some of them apparently ordinary people much like you and me, who try to identify the extracts and then discuss them. So far, since I've been watching, it's turned out that almost all the panel have read almost every book which has come up, not to mention all the author's other works as well.

But I haven't read a single one of them. Not a solitary book that's been mentioned on the programme since I've been watching have I read.

I sit in front of the darkened set long after the programme has finished, sunk into a melancholic trance, waiting for my wife to talk me back to a state of reason.

"You may not have read the books," she says, "but you guessed some of them. Or at any rate, you almost guessed some of them. Now that really *is* an achievement, almost guessing a book you haven't read."

I groan faintly.

"That bit of Kafka that none of them knew—as soon as the word 'Kafka' came up on the screen you shouted 'Christ! I was going to say Capek! I got the right country!'"

"I shouted that, did I?"

"Certainly you did. I'm sure you'd have got a lot more right if you hadn't had to jump up and shout it out so hurriedly before the title came up on the screen."

"What about the time I shouted 'Charlotte Brontë!' and it turned out to be Rider Haggard?"

"Everyone makes mistakes. But what about the time you shouted '1984!' and it turned out to be 'Brave New World'? That was very close."

"I meant to shout 'Brave New World,' as a matter of fact."

"So you kept shouting afterwards."

"I got over-excited. Shouted the wrong word."

"Exactly. You were terribly good. And even if you hadn't read any of the books, you'd read reviews of some of them."

"Oh, I'd read *reviews* of some of them."

"Anyway, there's reading and reading. I expect this lot just skim through books at great speed, without really taking them in at all. Now when you read you really *read*. You frown. You breathe hard. You take an extremely long time to get through a page."

"Don't tell me."

"It took you nine months to read 'War and Peace.'"

"I was an old man by the time I'd finished."

"And six months of travelling back and forth between London and Manchester, with sleepless nights on the sleeper and interminable hours waiting for delayed planes, to get through 'Ulysses.' Now that's what I *call* reading."

"Have I read 'Ulysses'?"

"Certainly you have."

"Ah. That's one that might well come up on the programme."

"Exactly."

"About a man in Dublin, is it? Kind of stream of consciousness?"

"That's right—with a green cover. That's what I mean. All that lot tore through 'Ulysses' one wet games afternoon in the fourth form. But when *you* read a book it really gets right down into your subconscious like some infantile trauma. You can't remember a word of it."

"That's true."

"Anyway, you know all about all sorts of things they don't. You know about Wittgenstein, and—well—Wittgenstein . . ."

"Oh God, so do they!"

"That lot? Know about Wittgenstein? Don't make me laugh."

"You really think they don't?"

"They don't know the first thing about him."

"Seriously?"

"Seriously."

"No, they know about Wittgenstein all right. You can't get away from it—I simply don't read enough books."

"You've read at least four this year."

"They were only paperbacks."

"They were the paperbacks of the hardbacks everyone said were the best books of the year."

"Yes—of the year before last."

"You're only two years behind."

"I'm slipping further back all the time. At this rate I won't be reading this year's books until 1970."

"Why don't you miss out a year or two? Otherwise you're only going to be getting round to books just as everyone realises how bad they are after all. You know how that depresses you."

"But what about the backlog from earlier years?"

"You mean Defoe and Smollett and Richardson?"

"Exactly."

"And Johnson's Lives of the Poets, and Boswell's Life of Johnson, and Carlyle's essay on Boswell, and Froude's Life of Carlyle...?"

"That's enough. Don't run on about it."

"Couldn't you skip, like everybody else?"

"Skip? Me? With my completion neurosis?"

"Well, couldn't you possibly start reading now, instead of just talking about it?"

"What? With my depression syndrome?"

"Oh well, never mind. One of these days they'll do a book you've read."

Between the Acts

"Hey, Fred!" screams Ed. "It's Ted! He's dead!"

Blackout. Curtain. Interval.

Ah, the interval! O blessed season! Now I will lift up my voice and praise this happy time.

"Hot in there."

"Yes."

"Hot out here, too."

"Yes."

Gaze about at furnishings. Find self standing in front of poster for play inside saying: *Most important theatrical event of the decade.*—*O. J. Sprout*. Study words at leisure for some minutes.

"Are you enjoying it?"

"Oh yes. I think so. Are you?"

"Oh tremendously. In a way."

"Strong curtain, I thought."

"Yes. Good act. In a way."

"Yes."

Look down at feet. Try to turn them out at angle of 180 degrees. Minor obsession of mine.

"Want a drink?"

"Had a drink in the last interval, didn't we?"

"I suppose we did."

"Anyway, the bar's crowded."

Return to contemplation of foot drill for a while.

"I liked that bit where Ed sort of leered at Fred."

"*Yes!*"

"And that bit where Ted sort of said sort of 'Well, go on and butter the sodding bread,' sort of thing."

"That was marvellous."

Examine feet for a little, until eye falls on poster saying *An evening of continuous bliss.*—*J. Lambert Trouncer*. Examine that for a time instead.

"And that bit where Fred sort of screeched 'Ted!'"

"Which bit was that?"

"You know, the bit where Ted was on the bed."

"Oh, he didn't say Ted. He said Ed. That was the point. He knew it was Ted, but he called him Ed."

"Oh, I *see*."

"I think that was the point, wasn't it?"

"I must admit, I didn't get that at all."

"Oh, I think that was the marvellous thing about it."

Pivot right heel on welt of left shoe. See how far can turn it before it comes unhinged. Feeble, feeble. Try again....

"You don't think it's time to go back?"

"Don't think the bell's gone yet, has it?"

Funny, welt on right shoe seems to be wider than welt on left shoe. Must be imagination. Try controlled programme of five swings on each welt.

"And that bit where Fred sort of tapped Ed on the head!"

"Um?"

"I said that bit where Fred sort of tapped Ed on the head!"

"Oh, *marvellous*! Sorry—I was trying to hear what that couple just behind me were saying. She looks exactly like a girl I was at school with."

Now a more difficult trick. Turn right foot completely round, so that it lies toe to heel and heel to toe against left one. Agh! Stagger slightly against poster saying *I loved every minute.—K. D. Haddock.*

"Terribly funny bit where he sort of kicked his old father sort of down the stairs."

"You thought that was funny?"

"You didn't?"

"Well, yes and no. I must admit, it worried me a bit."

"You mean, the sort of idea of kicking one's...?"

"Well, just a *bit*."

"I see what you mean."

"I mean, I thought it was in a sense sort of tremendously funny."

"Sort of black comedy, I thought."

"Oh, the whole thing. Pitch black."

"Yes. The bell hasn't gone yet, has it?"

Now going to attempt the most difficult trick of all—aligning feet at 180 degrees with toes in and heels out.

"I mean, it doesn't make one *laugh*."

"Oh God no."

"I mean, if anything, one's sort of bored."

"Fantastically bored."

"Sort of alienation effect."

"Yes. I mean, in a way the whole thing's absolutely sort of cretinous."

"That's what's so good about it. Isn't it?"

Sure I can get these damned feet inside out if I really put my mind to it. . . .

"For God's sake—everyone's staring."

"What? Oh, sorry."

"Oughtn't we to be getting back?"

"Don't want to get back too soon, do we?"

Start to balance left heel on top of right toe, recollect self, and quickly put it back in its place, now curiously occupied by another theatre-lover's foot.

"Sorry."

"Sorry."

Stand perfectly still, eyes glued on *I loved every minute*.

"Ah, *there* goes the bell."

Darkness. Curtain up.

"Dead, Ed?" says Fred. "Not Ted?"

Lord, receive us with Thy blessing, Once again assembled here....

H.I.5

In the peeling, anonymous lobby, Costello showed his pass to the security man. He took a lift to the fourth floor, showed his pass again, and went straight to Control's office, the advance copy of the List still in his hand.

"I'll tell him you're here," said Control's pretty secretary, giving him a specially sympathetic smile. No doubt everyone would give him a specially sympathetic smile today. One of his best men was blown; already it was vaguely known in the office that he had put up some sort of black. He kept his face wooden.

"Would you go in?" said the pretty secretary, smiling again.

It was hot inside Control's office. Probably the window latch was broken, like everything else in the room. Control sat visibly sweating in his tweed suit, mortifying his flesh by removing neither jacket nor waistcoat. A cup of ancient office tea stood on his copy of the Birthday Honours List. It had left several wet rings on the Companions of Honour, Costello noticed.

"I'm sorry about Spode," said Control, nodding at the List.

"Yes," said Costello flatly.

"Doing a drunk driving on you like that, after you'd cleared him up to K.C.M.G. level. We only just got him out in time"

"Yes."

"Three others in the last couple of years, weren't there, who went down one way or another? One for embezzling, one co-respondent, and one who defected to the Russians?"

"Yes."

"It doesn't look too good, you know. The Committee don't like it."

"Naturally not."

"I only mention it. No use crying over spilt milk, of course. We've got to get down to the next batch for the New Year list. I'm putting you down to do a chap called Sneame—G. B. J. Sneame. He's been Head Gardener at the British Hospital in Zurich for 37 years. Roughboys, the Director, nominated him."

"A head gardener? You mean, for an M.B.E.?"

"Now I don't want you to think of this as a demotion, Costello."

"But I've been doing Mike and Georges for 10 years now."

"The Committee feels you'd benefit from vetting a few M.B.E. nominations again. You know, Costello, in Honours Intelligence we don't think any less of a man because he's only been nominated for the M.B.E. After all, he's a human being just like you and me. I believe we should remember that an M.B.E., a G.C.M.G.—even a K.G.—are all equal in the sight of God."

"Yes. You want me to find out if this man's any good at gardening?"

"Oh, he's *good* all right. We know that much. You'll find it all on the file. But is he *damned* good? That's what we want to know. Is he *M.B.E.* good?"

"All right."

"I want you to go out there as a representative of a firm selling specialised pesticides. I take it you can handle a spray-gun if the need arises?"

"Yes."

"Take a look at his roses, Costello. That's the kind of thing the Committee wants to know about. Is he growing first-class English roses out there, with good size, colour, and scent? Is he free of aphis? Has he kept his nose clean on slugs? That's the kind of stuff I can make out a case with. Roughboys says he's strong on miniature cactus. The Committee doesn't want to know about his miniature cactus, Costello, or his pond-weed or his herb-garden. You can't give a man the M.B.E. for growing pots of miniature cactus. Do you see what I mean?"

"I've done M.B.E.s before, Control."

"You've been off them for years. Don't forget that."

"I shan't forget it."

"Roses, Costello. It's absolutely vital that we should know the truth about Sneame's roses."

Control took a reflective sip of cold tea.

"We'd need photographs, Costello—blueprints—actual measurements. Look, what we want to know is the strategic effect of these roses. Is this man filling the whole of Zurich with the unmistakable perfume of an English rose-garden all summer? Is he making Englishmen in Zurich step a little more proudly? Is he making hard-headed Swiss buyers dream of business trips to Britain? We could pay for information like that, Costello?"

"Just leave it to me."

Control gazed at the tea-stained Honours List for some minutes, playing with a broken stapling machine.

"Then again," he said, "we'd need to know what sort of man he is. A loyal worker. But how loyal? Has he ever asked for a rise?"

"Look, I did 20 gardeners for M.B.E.s in my first year down from Oxford."

"Roughboys says he's unfailingly cheerful. How cheerful is that, Costello? Does he have a smile for everyone? Including the Swiss? Or does he just grin sycophantically at Roughboys and the senior surgeons? *Exactly* how many times a day does he smile? How many times does he laugh? Does he whistle a merry tune as he dungs those roses, Costello? Or does he just produce a tuneless noise that gets on everybody's nerves?"

"I'll measure the exact pitch, Control."

"And another thing. Find out how many arms and legs he's got. Even if the roses all had green-fly and he only forced a grin on pay-day we could probably swing it if he was a leg or two short.".

"I'll count up, Control. You know I always do."

"All right, then. But Costello. Take care on this one, will you? Just remember I'm nominated for the K.C.B. myself in this next lot."

Hommes de Plume

One of the most disconcerting things about getting older is that you become more naïve and gullible all the time. Every year you get a little less knowledgeable, a little less worldly-wise.

Well, I say *you* do. *I* do. I reached my peak of worldly wisdom round about the age of 17. You'd have had to get up very early in the morning to pull the wool over my eyes in those days. I knew that nothing was what it appeared to be in this world, that it was really all fixed behind the scenes by the Great Conspiracy—Krupp, the United Fruit Company, Vickers Armstrong, and the rest of them. I knew that the newspapers, the Government, and everything else was just a façade. A fellow I met in a Youth Hostel told me.

There were other kids in the school who were equally certain that the Great Conspiracy taking over everywhere was operated by the Comintern, Konni Zilliacus, and Sir Stafford Cripps. These points of detail divided us at the time, but I see now that fundamentally we'd got hold of the same idea.

And yet, as the years went by, all that bright plating of worldly wisdom began to wear off. In some cases, I came to see, one was pretty well forced to the conclusion that to a certain limited extent things were more or less what they appeared to be—up to a point, with reservations.

I only realise quite how naïve and credulous I've become these days when I meet young people who have the bloom of worldly wisdom still upon them. They're not fooled—they're not fooled by *me* for a start. Do I really say what I think in my articles? they ask, with that coolly sceptical look in their eye that I once had in mine. Do I really intend what I say to be taken seriously?

The breadth and sweep of their scepticism disconcerts me. I shuffle about guiltily, looking more and more like a front-man for the Communists or a hireling of the international steel cartels every minute. "Well, er, yes," I mumble. "Er, yes, I kind of do. I mean, not for any lofty motives, of course—just to avoid the sheer unnecessary labour of thinking up two completely different sets of opinions."

. They smile disbelievingly. They know I have to say this. Some of them break the conversation off at this point, their worst suspicions confirmed already. But the real hard core go on to ask if I actually write my own stuff.

I don't know whether all journalists are asked this, or whether there's something especially shifty about me. But the question has been put to me about once a month since I first started to write articles in newspapers, and each time it comes up I get the same sensation of vertigo, of being suspended above such an abyss of mutual incomprehension that I daren't even think about it.

As a matter of fact, it's even worse if you appear on television. The sight of someone actually speaking his words in person seems to lead even quite old people to assume that those words must have been put into his mouth by faceless men behind the scenes. I point out, falteringly, that if somebody else wrote the stuff, that same somebody else would get the money for it, and I'd starve. They grin, frankly amused to think I expect them to believe such kids' stuff.

I tell you, over the years this single-minded interrogation is beginning to break me down. I don't think I can stand up to psychological pressures like this any longer.

All right—I'll come clean. I don't write my stuff at all. It's the Great Conspiracy at work once again—the C.I.A., the London merchant bankers, the Union Minière, the Soviet Chief Intelligence Directorate. . . .

(Caught some of you looking momentarily startled there, didn't I? What? You don't still think the world Communist conspiracy's something separate, do you? Hey, lads, there's a kid here who didn't know the Soviet spy network and the C.I.A. were all part of the same organisation! Don't worry, son, you'll grow up one day.)

Yes, I confess, all my stuff is written by a man called Mott—R. D. Mott. Doesn't look particularly sinister, but then these people never do, of course. Thick glasses, receding hairline—slightly moth-eaten literary man. I met him at a party the other night.

"I've always wanted to meet you," I said. "I must say, I've rather enjoyed one or two of my pieces."

"Oh, thanks," he said, smirking unbecomingly. "That's very kind of you."

"Thought I'd got one or two quite pretty turns of phrase here and there. One thing I've always wanted to ask you, though—do you actually write my stuff yourself?"

Well, he stammered and shifted from foot to foot and gave me a lot of rubbish about how he had to write it, or the *Observer* wouldn't pay him for it, but I just smiled sarcastically.

"Ah, come on," I said. "I wasn't born yesterday. I know it's all fixed up behind the scenes."

"Look," he shouted. "Who's writing the piece we're in at the moment—you or me?"

"Not you, evidently," I replied. "I seem to be making you look a complete fool. It's obviously some more sinister figure further back still, trying to discredit both of us."

He thought about this for a bit.

"All right," he said. "I'll be frank with you. I don't really write your stuff at all. It's knocked out by a man called Kreisler—K. L. K. Kreisler. Quite a pleasant sort of fellow, in a rather boorish way. Half-German—wears Adhite shoes."

But this didn't take me in for a moment.

"If it were Kreisler putting these words in our mouth," I said, "you don't really think he'd have mentioned his Adhite shoes, do you?"

"You mean," said Mott, "there's someone behind Kreisler...?"

We'll track it down eventually. Probably to some milk-and-water Sunday-school teacher in Ealing with a duelling scar under his toupée....

Tête-à-Tête-à-Tête

"What do you feel about the passing of the shirt tail?" asked my wife suddenly the other day, in a thoughtful tone of voice. If only I'd had the presence of mind to reply:—

"I personally—and of course you will understand that I am speaking now purely as an individual—I personally believe that the passing of the shirt tail is something deeply symptomatic of the social crisis of our times—and one to which all too little attention has been paid by the Press and the public alike."

If I'd managed to say that, we should at last have had the makings of a *television conversation* in our own home. We should have shown that it was possible for ordinary people to emancipate themselves from the old-fashioned private conversation, intended merely as a utilitarian form of communication between those taking part, and to aspire to the new public conversation, held exclusively in order to be overheard. To take an analogy from another art, we should have moved in one step from singing in the bath to the mad scene from *Lucia di Lammermoor*. If not farther.

Well, it will come, it will come. And when it does, my wife can scarcely help but reply:—

"I think I'm right in saying, am I not, that to you a shirt which comes untucked from the top of your trousers is a very real symbol of the chaos and violence eternally present beneath the surface of life?"

Self: Yes, I think this symbolism has been a constant theme in my work over the last 10 years—almost an obsession. To me the shirt that comes untucked is the eternal artist and rebel—the Rimbaud, the Raskolnikov—if you like, the Wild One on the beach at Margate—who breaks loose from surroundings he finds intolerably restrictive, and in so doing shows up the hollow pretensions of the trousers from which he has escaped.

Wife: This is of course, is it not, a theme which has fascinated and inspired artists ever since the invention of the trouser? But what I think many people may not realise is that, *paradoxically*, in your personal life you yourself have made—and indeed to my knowledge still make—the most enormous, one might almost say the most *gigantic*, efforts to keep your own shirt tucked in.

Self: I think this ambivalence, this one might almost say *dichotomy*, is very central, isn't it, is very seminal, to what I think it was C. S. Lewis would have called the noumenon, or as Jung so expressively put it, the mandala. Or, as we know it in our own lives, the shirt tail.

Wife: I remember—with enormous pleasure, if I may say so—the wonderful exhibition you made of yourself with an untucked shirt at Edinburgh in 1961. I hope we shall have a chance to see that performance repeated some time in the very near future.

Self: Thank you. And now, to change the subject. It's a far cry from shirt tails to bath-water, but all the same, it's bath-water that we're going to talk about now. I think we were all shocked to hear the news today that the bath belonging to our good friends Horace and Doris Morris had overflowed. Now, I believe you were in the area recently, shortly before the flooding occurred. Can you say anything which would help me to evaluate the scale of the disaster?

Wife: Well, the bathroom is about 15 ft long by 10 ft wide, with important towel-drying installations on the south side and dense clumps of toothbrush on the north. But I should imagine that the area which was chiefly affected was the floor, which as I remember it was comparatively low-lying.

Self: As one who knows the Morrises intimately, how do you think they will react to the situation?

Wife: Well, knowing them as I do, and indeed as you do, I believe they will pull together—make a really tremendous united effort to get the damage repaired and put their bathroom back into commission as soon as possible.

Self: Well, we wish them luck. From bath-water it's but a short step to another liquid—tea. I'm going to pass you a cup of tea. Here it is—a cup of tea. Just an ordinary cup, with tea inside it. Now I want you to look at this cup of tea, at this perfectly ordinary cup, with this perfectly ordinary tea inside it, and tell me if you would like sugar in it.

Wife: Just one lump, please, of perfectly ordinary sugar. And from a lump of sugar we move many thousands of miles northwards, from the sugar plantations of Trinidad to these rather less sunny climes—to a lump in the throat here at home. To the lump in the throat, to be precise, without which I cannot recall the time when I was single.

Self: Perhaps I should just interrupt here, if I may, to make it clear that you are now married.

Wife: That is correct.

Self: And what I think is quite interesting to note—and I believe this is something you are too modest to mention—you are in fact married to me.

Wife: Yes, I think that's a point worth making. Anyway, as I was saying, I cannot recall without emotion the time when I was single, and had no one with whom to hold a conversation and share my inmost thoughts.

Self: I know this is a painful question, and believe me, I would not ask it if I did not have to in order to get the answer I need to round off this unscripted, spontaneous discussion. What did you do for conversation in those days?

Wife: I just gazed sadly into the teleprompter and talked to myself.

Self: Mrs. Frayn—thank you.

Ivan Kudovbin

It's a weirdly fascinating business watching sober and fair-minded human beings trying to work out a formula for the circumstances in which abortion should be permitted. All possible reasons and permutations of reasons are canvassed and debated; excepting only the reason that the woman concerned wants an abortion, which no one mentions as having any relevance to the question at all.

Of course, this way of thinking is very congenial to a bureaucracy-loving socialist like me, who believes that people shouldn't be allowed any freedom to choose for themselves, but should have all their decisions made for them by faceless officials and so-called experts who think they know what's best for everyone. But I'm rather surprised that the tireless defenders of personal liberty whom we usually find ourselves up against in our insidious erosion of citizen rights haven't been exposing controls and snoopers in this sector with quite their usual vigour.

No, I was being gently ironical. I'm aware that those who deny that a pregnant woman has any personal right to choose whether she wants to give birth do so because they are trying to protect the right of the unborn to be born. And there are two arguments often advanced in this direction which I must admit I find rather compelling.

The first is that few people (if any), once having got themselves born and in a position to say, would prefer not to have been born, however reluctant or unsuitable their mother, or however exhausted and inadequate she subsequently became. The second (and logically similar) argument is that if abortion had been freely available in the past, the world might have been deprived of individuals like Leonardo da Vinci and William the Conqueror (who were illegitimate), and Bach (the eighth of eight children).

These arguments are good ones. The only trouble with them is that they're *too* good. Take the case of that astonishing sixteenth-century figure Ivan Kudovbin. He invented a primitive form of gas-mantle; he wrote 123 flute sonatas, before the sonata form had been invented; he experimented with cheap money and deficit budgeting; he raised a citizen army which drove the Galicians right out of Galicia into Silesia, and the Silesians right out of Silesia into Galicia. He was undoubtedly a genius. But, as we know from studying the history of the period, he was one of the unlucky ones who didn't get born. He Kudovbin, but he wasn't. If he *had* been born he would have preferred to have been born, I'm pretty sure. His loss is a tragedy both to himself and to mankind.

Perhaps Kudovbin was aborted or miscarried—I'm not sure. But I think the trouble was quite probably that he never got conceived. I don't know what went wrong exactly. Perhaps he was the twelfth child in the family, and his parents stopped at eleven. Perhaps his mother was a nun, under vows of chastity. Perhaps his father was away on a business trip the night he should have been commenced. But what seems fairly certain mathematically is that the tragedy of his non-birth could have been averted if everyone had really taken the matter seriously.

Think of it. If the available reproductive plant had been fully utilised from the beginning of time, and every woman had been kept bearing a child a year from puberty to menopause, billions upon billions more people would have been born. Nearly all of them, once born, would have preferred to have been born. And among them, presumably, would have been the usual proportion of geniuses. Kudovbin after Kudovbin— composers who wrote greater polyphonic music than Bach; Elizabethan dramatists more universal than Shakespeare; Elizabethan monarchs more Elizabethan than Elizabeth.

The steamboat would have been invented in time to take people to the Crusades; the United Nations in time to reach a negotiated settlement instead. Frozen fish-fingers would have come in about the beginning of the Renaissance.

Just think for a start how many innocent babes—potential great men among them—have been kept out of this world because of legal or moral sanctions against fornication, adultery, rape, and intercourse below the age of consent! Sentimentalists have opposed these creative and life-enhancing activities on various short-sighted grounds, such as the well-being of the woman concerned, and the desirability of stable family and social life. Have they ever stopped to consider the well-being of poor little Vsevolod and Tatiana Kudovbin, who as a result of their interference never even started being, well or ill?

But then, people never stop to think about the rights of the unborn. So-called reformers struggled for years to get slavery abolished, using a variety of spurious moral arguments, but really on the shallow hedonistic grounds that the slaves themselves didn't much care for it. Didn't they, indeed! Nobody stopped to consider that without slavery there would in years to come be no Buddy Bolden, no Jelly Roll Morton, no Blind Lemon Jefferson; hence no syncopated popular music of any sort; hence no Beatles and no Cilla Black. So much for Cilla Black, for all Wilberforce cared.

The simple truth is, that it's an ill wind that blows nobody any silver linings. So carry on persecuting people; they may be Dostoyevsky. And don't hesitate to martyr any likely-looking candidate; remember, he may not get canonised otherwise.

Cottage Industry

The wonderful thing about having a country cottage, say our good friends Christopher and Lavinia Crumble, is that they can have their good friends (such as us) down for the weekend.

"And the wonderful thing about having our friends down for the weekend," explains Lavinia, as they take our bags and show us our room, "is that we really have the chance to *talk* to them down here, away from all the mad rush of town life. Don't we, darling?"

"We like to feel we've created a setting for the sort of relaxed house-party thing that used to be such an important part of the civilised way of life in the past," says Christopher. "Plain living and high thinking—that kind of thing. We find ourselves talking like *mad* down here. Don't we, darling?"

Apparently the place was absolutely derelict when they found it. All their friends thought they were *crazy*. But of course they got it for a song, and they did it all up themselves.

"We really have put a tremendous amount of work into it. Haven't we, darling?"

"People think we've been spending our weekends idling about in the countryside. But we've scarcely had time to sit down! You really can't imagine how much we've had to do. Can they, darling?"

Apparently *all* the beams we can now see were covered with plaster and wallpaper when they moved in! The doorway we've just come through didn't *exist*! The floor we're now standing on was *completely* rotten! The whole house *reeked* of mildew! We can't really appreciate its present condition, of course, not having seen it in its original state.

"I mean, Christopher did have a tiny worry when we bought it that we might be doing local people out of a house. You know what Christopher's like! But it was absolutely *dere-lict....*"

"And of course what these people want is really some neat little two-up-and-two-down semi. Isn't it, darling?"

"And if we hadn't done it up somebody else would have. Wouldn't they, darling?"

"They're not all as tender-hearted as we are. And we have put the most tremendous amount of work into the place."

Have we admired their view, they ask? Oh, God, the view—no, we haven't. Admire, admire. Only six miles or so beyond that electricity sub-station, apparently, is the Vale of Relpham, which Walter Bridmore mentions in one of his novels! The window-frame itself, it appears, is treated with Osterman's "Windowjoy" polyester window-frame sealer.

They expect we'd like a wash etcetera after our journey. It seems terrible to interrupt our discussion of architecture and literature for anything so mundane as a wash etcetera. But there's plenty for us to admire and meditate upon in the bathroom. Apparently Christopher did most of the plumbing himself, and is rather proud of his handiwork. And we're to help ourselves to hot water as lavishly as we like, because they've installed a Supa-Heata, the literature about which we must remind them to give us before we go.

Over lunch the conversation turns to the world of art.

"Did you admire that old Agricultural Show poster in the loo?" inquires Christopher. "We're frightfully proud of it. Lavinia got it from a little man over in Market Strayborough. Didn't you, darling?"

"Of course, the loo's our great triumph altogether. I found a little man in Morton Winchevers who built us the septic tank for about half what we'd have had to pay a big firm."

"And she found another little man practically next door to the little man in Market Strayborough who got hold of that Victorian pedestal and cistern for us. Lavinia's got an absolute genius for getting hold of little men. Haven't you, darling?"

In the afternoon we go for a stroll, so that our hosts can point out various features of the locality of which they're particularly proud, and introduce us to one or two *marvellous* locals we absolutely must meet, now that the Crumbles have succeeded by dint of hard work and perseverance in penetrating their natural rural reserve. The long grass in the meadows and the summery smell of the cow-parsley along the lanes put everyone in a gently reflective mood.

"You can get down here in 4½ hours, you know," says Christopher, "if you avoid Snaith, and take that little road through Chocking which comes out just this side of Griever...."

"Or 4¼, if you don't get held up by all that terrible weekend traffic to the coast where you cross the main road at West-champs Peverel...."

"Which is awfully good, you know, when you think about it. It means that we can leave here at half-past four on a Monday morning, and be in our respective offices by nine...."

Tea on the lawn, of course, sparks off an earnest debate on the nature of lawns in general, and of Christopher's efforts upon this one in particular, which we gather are beyond all praise, given the patch of thistles and nettles he had to start with.

Night comes down, obscuring the lawn wrested with such difficulty from the weeds, and the much-discussed patch of earth which Lavinia hasn't yet decided whether to fill with orodigia or flowering pangloss, and the blue paintwork on the doors and windows (Luxibrite's Melanesian Blue, which they think—and we definitely agree—is a much more subtle colour than Housallure's Gulfstream or Goyamel's Stratosphere); making the peripatetic conversationalists on the terrace only shadowy shapes as they murmur on into the dusk.

"I'll put the terrace light on. No, no—no trouble at all. We're rather proud of our electric lighting, as a matter of fact. Aren't we, darling?"

"Honestly, you'd never believe the struggle we had to get this place on the supply. It seems a pity not to use it, now we've got it. Doesn't it, darling?"

Yes, it's wonderful, as the Crumbles say, to get away from the dreadful rat-race in town for a day or two, and take a look at the one in the country for a change.

Spock's Guide to Parent Care

PARENTS ARE JUST LARGE HUMAN BEINGS. It's only natural for a small child to feel a little daunted by the hard work and responsibility of coping with parents. All parents get balky from time to time, and go through phases which worry their children, and all children get tired and discouraged and wonder whether they're doing the right thing.

The important thing to remember is that most parents, deep down inside, want nothing more than to be good ones. A parent may act tough and cocky, but at heart he wants to be one of the gang. He wants to learn what's expected of him as a parent and do it. What he needs from you above all is plenty of encouragement, and plenty of reassurance that he's doing all right.

EVERY PARENT IS DIFFERENT. This one flies into a fury at the sight of crayoning on the wallpaper. That one bursts into tears. Yet another goes into a sulk and won't say anything all afternoon. All these are perfectly normal, healthy reactions. I'd be inclined to be suspicious of the parent who seems a little too good to be true. He or she may be deprived of emotional experience for lack of opportunity. I think I'd ask myself in this case if I was drawing on the wallpaper enough.

THEY AREN'T AS FRAGILE AS THEY LOOK. Handle them confidently. Many parents look as though they'll have a nervous breakdown if you bang your toy on the table just once more. Don't worry—nine times out of ten they won't.

DON'T BE AFRAID TO INSIST ON YOUR OWN STANDARDS. There's been a great swing away from the overpermissiveness which used to be the fashion, when a parent's every whim was regarded as sacred. Nowadays we've come to realise that on the whole people don't have any very clear ideas about manners or morals until they become parents, when they hastily start to make them up as they go along. They're secretly very grateful for a little firm but tactful guidance.

I don't mean by this that you should squash the parents' own spontaneous efforts to help. But what they eventually learn to think right and proper will be decided very largely by the way you act anyhow.

PLAY IS EDUCATION, TOO. All the time you are with your parents you are educating them in tolerance and self-discipline. Playing games and romping with them is specially useful. It's not only great fun for them—it's helping to form their characters. Various games such as hitting your little brother, and then bursting into tears before he does, train their powers of detection and judgment. Jumping on their stomachs after meals and finding reasons to get them up in the middle of the night develop their resistance to hardship, and generate a sense of righteousness which will enable them to face cheating their colleagues next day with an easy conscience.

TEMPER TANTRUMS. Almost all parents have temper tantrums from time to time. You have to remember that between the ages of 20 and 60 parents are going through a difficult phase of their development. They have got to a stage in their exploration of the world at which they find it is rather smaller than they thought. They are discovering the surprising limitations of their personality, and learning to be dependent. It's natural enough for them to want to explode at times.

It's no use arguing with a parent who's in this sort of state. The best thing is just to let him cool off. But you might try to distract him and offer him a graceful way out by suggesting something that's fun to do, like taking it out of your little brother instead.

GO EASY ON KIDDING. Most parents enjoy a joke. If you get hold of a good one, try it on them 20 or 30 times, just to show them what it's like being on the receiving end of the family's sense of humour. But I think I'd give it a rest after that, in case it causes nightmares.

JEALOUSY. Most parents are worried, though they probably wouldn't admit it, that they're not really good enough, and that other parents are better at the job than they are. In one parent it will take the form of worrying that his children are not as pretty, or as well-behaved, or as intelligent as other people's. Another will try to resolve his fears by telling himself that other parents don't really look after their children properly.

A parent showing symptoms of jealousy needs lots of love and reassurance. Once in a while it might help to beat the boy next door in a clean fight, or win that scholarship. But you can't do this too often without the risk of spoiling the parent. Once a parent gets the idea that he can just sulk and you'll win a scholarship for him he'll lead you a terrible dance.

BE FRIENDLY BUT FIRM. In general, don't give your parents too much chance to argue. Just quietly get on with whatever you want to do, perhaps chatting amiably to distract their attention. The chances are they won't even notice, or that when they do it will be too late for them to feel like making a fuss.

Parents can sometimes drive a small child almost to distraction by dawdling about in shops, or talking to friends. It doesn't really help to keep nagging, or to try dragging them along by brute force. If I were you I'd hop cheerfully about from foot to foot, and say in a firm, friendly voice: "I want to go to the lavatory." If that doesn't work, you could try turning white, and saying you're going to be sick.

REMEMBER, YOU'RE HELPING THEM TO GROW UP. It's your job to help your parents grow up into mature, responsible old-age pensioners, self-confident, armed with a workable code of morals and manners, and too exhausted in mind and body to make trouble for anyone else. If you keep in mind that you're training your children's grandparents you won't go far wrong.

What the Mice Foretell

The ancients tried to unriddle the secrets of the universe by an extraordinary variety of techniques, such as, according to Roget's Thesaurus, hieromancy and icthyomancy (examining the entrails of animals and fishes), austromancy and crithomancy (studying the winds and the dough of cakes), and myomancy (for those who preferred a little flutter on the mice).

These barbarous superstitions seem inconceivably remote from us today. Who can imagine any modern statesman resorting to crithomancy, and waiting, before he took action, to see exactly how the cookie crumbled? Or turning in his difficulties to austromancy, and not committing himself until he'd found out which way the wind was blowing?

In those far-off days they used to resolve their problems by balancing a hatchet (axinomancy), and by going round in circles (gyromancy). Picture President Johnson juggling with weapons in the face of a crisis! Or Mr. Wilson gyromancing uncertainly about! The mere idea is enough to make one provide material for geloscopy, which is divination by the mode of laughing.

Nowadays we do it differently, as I can tell you from personal experience. We journalists are the real augurs and haruspices of the modern world, ready at all hours with prognostications and divinations at popular prices. We don't use mice or dough, I can tell you, and we shouldn't so much as glance at the intestines of a holy pig if you laid them out in front of us.

We rely on much more advanced systems, such as taximancy, shrdlumancy, and freudomancy. Thus, taximancy teaches us that the views of one taxi-driver picked off the rank at random to drive us in from the airport are more significant than any systematic survey of opinion. Because, in sending us that particular taxi-driver with that particular set of opinions, the gods, or the Norns, or at any rate the taxi-dispatchers, are clearly trying to get some message through to us.

According to freudomancy, moments of misunderstanding and error offer us flashes of illumination from the Collective Unconscious which are unobtainable through regular channels. Misprints, similarly, are more revealing than something printed correctly; instead of a communication from some mortal author, we are vouchsafed a direct message from Shrdlu, the dark but playful god who lurks at every compositor's fingertips. And in general, what almost happened, and what one for a moment thought someone was about to say, is more telling than what actually did happen or got said.

The theory is abstruse; the practice is entirely straightforward. For instance, in a recent book about the situation of the writer in America, among other places, A. Alvarez reports that he woke up as his plane approached New York just in time to hear the cabin loudspeaker say, "This is John F. Kennedy." In the moments before he realised that this was the new name of Idlewild airport, Mr. Alvarez reaped a rich harvest of significant confusion—a "sense of being put off-centre in a macabre way—a sense of the absurd," which turned out after touchdown to pervade everything and everybody.

Mr. Alvarez is almost parsimonious in the use he makes of this ripe misunderstanding. If it had happened to me, I'd have made it support a chapter at least, and I'd have dined out on it every night before publication date into the bargain.

What happened to Mr. Alvarez after getting out of the aircraft I don't know, because all I've read of the book so far is the paragraph about John F. Kennedy, which was quoted in a review. Somehow it seemed quite significant enough on its own. (This is what the ancients called *stichomancy*, or divination by passages in books.) But here's how I'd have gone on, if I'd been doing the job:—

"'Anything to declare?' asked the Customs man, and for a moment I had the wild feeling that I was expected to say something like 'Only that we hold these truths to be self-evident, that all men are created equal . . .' I didn't say it, of course, but it was an eerie experience, and the feeling persisted for a long time afterwards that this sort of lip-service to tradition was almost mandatory in America.

"I'd scarcely got into the arrivals lounge before I was practically hit in the eye by the sight of a slot-machine with the legend 'Gun 5 cents.' In fact it said '*Gum* 5 cents,' and the third leg of the m was simply hidden by the end of somebody's cigar. But I couldn't get over the feeling that it was in some way symptomatic of the violence always lurking just below the surface of American life, or that at any rate my reaction told me a great deal about the general jitteriness of people over there.

"What the driver of the airport bus thought about integration or violence or cultural pressures on the artist I don't know, because he said nothing at all throughout the trip, which with the best will in the world I couldn't help feeling suggested some profound fragmentation and failure of communication in American society.

"I walked from the town terminal to the cable office, and it was the little things I noticed most—the hardness and greyness of the pavement, a crumpled newspaper lying in a rubbish-bin, the folded raincoat over my arm. As far as the raincoat went, I felt I could be anywhere—Berlin 1932, Budapest 1956, Stockton-on-Tees 1965.

"I told the man at the cable office that I wanted to send this urgent news dispatch to London. For a moment I thought he was going to misunderstand me and assume I meant not London, England, but London, Ontario. He didn't; but for that split second I looked the grim old ghost of North American isolationism straight in the eye.

"(Next week: I see myself in the shaving-mirror at the Sherry-Netherland, and think for a moment it's Theodore Roosevelt.)"

Return Match

What really makes a holiday of course, is not the sun or the landscape or the architecture; it's the people.

It's the people who give a place its character, after all, and the intelligent holidaymaker makes a great effort to get to know them. They may be a bit shy at first, but you can be sure there's nothing they like more than a visitor really taking an interest in them. You stop and chat with them about their work. You find out how they live. You try to enter into the communal life of the place for a week or two. That's how real international understanding is created.

All the same, as I stroll about that delightful little unspoilt Psychomanian village chatting with the goatherds and dropping in for a glass of something with the old wattle-dauber, a worrying thought sometimes comes to me. Supposing they take it into their heads to get to know me back?

One day when I am back at home the front door bell is going to ring, and there on the doorstep will be a colourful Psychomanian peasant with his wrinkled wife, their wonderful timeless quality looking unpleasantly out of place among the sodium lights.

"Good morning!" he will say, with an ingratiating smile and irritatingly grammatical English. "Marvellous weather we're having, are we not?"

"Ah," I shall reply guardedly, my eyes narrowing with shrewd middle-class cautiousness.

"Of course, everyone knows the weather is never right for you townspeople! Ha, ha, ha! But the truth is, you people don't know how lucky you are to live in a suburb like this. The air's so thick and fumy—it's like wine. For poor devils like us who have to spend the rest of the year cooped up in the countryside breathing that thin country air it's as good as a tonic.

"I just dropped in to pass the time of day. Do you mind if I take a photograph of you as we talk? You look so typical, somehow, standing there in the door of your little home. . . . Head up, please. Look into the camera, will you, with that stupefied sort of expression? Thanks. Well, I expect you've got work to do."

"Yes."

"*Marvellous* accent," he whispers to his wife in Psychomanian.

"Honestly," he says to me, "don't worry about us. You just get on with your work and we'll watch you. No, truly, there's nothing I'd enjoy more."

When he discovers that I am an article writer by trade he is very excited.

"As a matter of fact," he says, "I'm by way of being something of a connoisseur of articles—I'm a member of the literary club at home, and we have regular article tastings. If you want my honest opinion, I'd swap any of your overpraised vintage Hazlitt and Addison for the sort of unpretentious rough stuff I expect you're turning out, if I could read it where it was meant to be read, in the rain, next to an English gasworks."

While his wife, who apparently doesn't speak English, goes out to the kitchen, smiling with wordless benevolence, to watch and make notes while my wife opens a tin of ravioli for lunch, he takes photographs of me operating the traditional typewriter. He asks me what all the different keys are for, and begs to be allowed to have a go himself.

"It looks easy when you do it," he says admiringly, as he

crashes his thick peasant fingers up and down. "But I can't seem to get any sort of article out of it at all."

"Takes practice," I mumble, flattered into loquacity.

"What a marvellously true thing to say! God, you people really have got a salty bourgeois wit, haven't you? How about singing one or two of your suburban songs for me? No? Well, then, what are the local superstitions round here? Do people hereabouts believe in little electrons, and all that sort of thing? Come on now—have you ever seen an electron yourself?"

I could tell him a thing or two about electrons all right, but I prefer to keep myself to myself, so I just shrug my shoulders and grunt expressively. With a little cry of delight the peasant discovers the telephone and asks if I would be prepared to sell it to him.

"I've got quite a little collection of English urban artefacts," he explains. "I find them rather amusing. Let's say a shilling, shall we?

"You know, it's a great privilege, being invited into such an ordinary home as this. But the really *marvellous* thing is to find oneself among people who've got time to sit down and talk. At home life is just one long rush to get the ground ploughed, the seed sown, the crop harvested. And of course it's a terrible rat-race, you know, the peasant world—everyone trying to be just that little bit shrewder and more obstinate than everyone else all the time.

"But then the whole pace of ancient life is killing. The trouble is, things are still so simple that there's nothing to think about but money, money, money. There are no chemicals in the bread—the eggs still taste like eggs—we plod senselessly from place to place at four miles an hour. I must say, I sometimes wonder where it will ever start.

"But it really is a wonderful break to sit here listening to you talk. You're so remote from the earth, somehow. Oh, is this ravioli for me? Gosh, thanks. Incidentally, I've heard a lot about the complex urban merry-making that goes on at cocktail parties. I don't know whether it would be possible to get into one?

"I mean, it is people who take one out of oneself on holiday, isn't it? And they cost so much less than all the other forms of entertainment I can think of."

At Bay in Gear Street

It's been hardly possible to get up and down Carnaby Street recently for the great crush of American journalists observing the swinging London scene. I was practically knocked down by a stampede of perspiring correspondents as I stepped out of Galt's toyshop the other day holding a doll I'd bought for the children.

"Holy heaven, it's Actor Terry Stamp, 26, in mini-wig and P.V.C. spectacles!" screamed the reporter from *Time* magazine. "And he's squiring diminutive dolly Cathy McGowan, 22, in an eight-inches-above-the-knee, Campari-red skirtlet, spectre-pale make-up, and kinky wobble-as-you-walk celluloid eyelids! I love you, Terry!"

"Are you crazy?" shouted the representative of *Status* magazine. "That's Jean Shrimpton in a trouser-suit, carrying Vidal Sassoon in newly groovy Now-We-Are-Six gear! Swinging, Shrimp, swinging!"

"No, listen!" cried the *Esquire* man, reading the label round the dolly's neck. "This is some new couple altogether called Non Toxic and Fully Washable! Hey, these are two totally unknown faces making the scene, boys!"

At this they all came crowding round, gazing at me and the doll as if they were going to eat us.

"Look at his trousers!" breathed the *Chicago Tribune*. "Two and a half inches above the shoe!"

"Two and three-quarter inches," said Associated Press, getting down on his hands and knees with a pocket rule.

"But only on the right leg!" pointed out N.B.C. excitedly. "The left trouser leg's practically trailing on the ground! Boys, this is the newest thing since yesterday, if not this morning!"

"And how about this—bags under the knees!" cried the *Daily News*. "Zowie! Back in New York they're still wearing their bags under the eyes! I tell you, these kids'll drive us into the sea!"

"Central button of jacket hanging on three-inch thread!" noted someone else.

"Two inches of shirt-tail worn· outside bellyband of trousers!"

"Neither of them are Negroes, have you noticed that? Pass the word back, men—Negroes are Out this afternoon."

"Sure—but short-sightedness is In, and so is shuffling the feet about and nervously blowing the nose."

Well, they all started shouting questions and trying to photograph me up the leg of my trousers. I gazed at them, stupefied.

"The guy can't understand," cried the *Wall Street Journal*. "Where the hell's the interpreter? Where's Jonathan Miller?"

"Leave it to me!" shouted *Time* magazine. "I know these people's patois."

He turned to me and the doll.

"Greetings, British bird and British Beatle!" he said very slowly, waving his hands about. "You—with it, yes? You— making scene, no?"

"*I'm* not making a scene," I replied nervously. "I was just suddenly set on by all you lot."

"He says he's set-on," reported *Time* magazine to the others. "That's the now-now-now phrase for switched-on."

" 'Set' spelt S-E-T and 'on' spelt O-N, Henry?" they asked him, writing it all carefully down.

"Hey, listen, boys! The dolly's saying something! What's she saying, Henry?"

"She's saying 'Mama.' "

" 'Mama' spelt M-A-M-A, Henry?"

"Right. What she's trying to get across is that today she is able to lead a deeply fulfilled life, thanks to the ready availability of artificial eyelashes and the policy of successive British Governments in granting independence to the country's overseas possessions."

They wrote it all down. I took advantage of the pause to explain that unfortunately I had to go.

" 'Go' is short for 'go, go, go,' of course," explained *Time* magazine. "I think what he's trying to say is that in this swinging new meritocratic young Britain the handsome young son of a peer can breeze up to the chemmy tables and lose a cool four or five hundred thousand dollars in a night as easily and naturally as the humblest mill-girl in Bolton."

"Where's he go-go-going to, Henry?" asked the *St. Louis Post-Dispatch*. "Annabel's? The Scotch?"

"British Beatle," translated *Time* magazine to me, "where you make the scene along towards?"

I said I was on my way to Oxford Circus Tube Station. They all looked it up on the map of The Scene in *Time*.

"It's not marked, Henry!" they cried.

"Don't worry, fellers—I know all about it. It'll be on the next edition of the map."

"What is it, Henry—a boutique or a discothèque?"

"It's a Tube station, men—'Tube' meaning 'groove,' of course. It's a sort of groovothèque."

"What kind of a set does he meet down there, Henry? Gamine Leslie Caron, 34? Ace Photographer David Bailey, 27? Or daughter of former Ambassador to the U.S. Lady Jane Ormsby-Gore, 23?"

I explained that the circle I moved in (though on the whole not in Oxford Circus Underground Station) consisted of Christopher and Lavinia Crumble, Horace and Doris Morris, and people like that. There were gasps of astonishment from the Press corps.

"Suffering saints!" they cried. "This is clearly some inner scene not as yet made by U.S. newsmen, which opens up entirely fresh dimensions of fabness, and brings within the reach of long-suffering mankind the hope of a whole gear universe of prime-quality grooviness!"

But just at that moment they saw Peter O'Toole coming by in bell-bottomed lederhosen and aluminium Boy Scout hat, and my fashionable career was over.

The dolly's been right off her food ever since.

Can You Hear Me, Mother?

I enjoy the woman's page of the *Guardian*. Unlike the men's pages of newspapers, where Interdepartmental Committees are Set Up, Machine Tool Prospects Look Brighter, and Proposals Deserve Careful Consideration, it seems to be concerned with individual human beings.

One has an impression of particular women, struggling with children and consciences and loose doorhandles; wondering gloomily whether it's God or madness tapping on their skulls: getting some strange illogical pleasure out of misconceived holiday ordeals with family, van, and tent through Wester Ross....

The other day the page made an even more striking excursion into the world of the personal and the particular; and I must say, the knife seemed to me to be getting a little near the bone.

It was an article by one Mair Thompson about mothers-in-law. Or, rather, about her own mother-in-law. One of the kindest and most generous people she knows, apparently, and she *loves* her.

"Yet she drives me crazy. Her mannerisms irritate me, her elderliness irritates me. I don't like her face, and her feet are silly-looking. Her conversation infuriates me. I let off steam by mimicking and muttering silently when she talks to me from another room. When she tells the same story for the umpteenth time it is with great difficulty that I restrain myself from either giggling or saying it along with her, word for word; I am amazed at my husband's ability to look interested and ask prompting questions."

I must admit, I felt the beads of nervous sweat start forth when I read this. I'm all for the unvarnished truth; I'm all for delivery by candour from inhibition and frustration. All the same—poor old mother-in-law! I take it that "Mair Thompson" is a pen-name.... I take it that mother-in-law never reads the *Guardian*.... But, all the same ...!

* * *

Of course, once you've got the problem into the open like this, everyone wants to help. Barbara Nuttall, of Leeds, writes to the *Guardian* to say that Mair Thompson's mother-in-law "ought gently to be told to come less often to her children's home." (Mrs. Nuttall's own mother-in-law "has never failed to help when needed," but at the same time "has never forced her attention" on the family.) But it's all the fault of the *husband*, according to Mrs. E. M. Selby, of Loughborough, who writes to say that "the weakness in the family structure mentioned lies more in the mother–son relationship. . . . The fact that the husband can sit patiently and listen to repetitive stories of his mother shows a childish dependence on her approval."

So poor old husband, too! It really is group therapy on the heroic scale, this candid assessment of one's relations' shortcomings in the public prints. Perhaps the impersonal abstractions of the men's pages have something to be said for them after all. I should certainly hate to pick up the paper one morning when my children were grown up and find some son-in-law of mine holding forth about me in the middle of the business news.

"A finer man than my father-in-law never drew breath," I can imagine the young puppy declaring sententiously, "when it comes to washing-up, carrying messages, waiting at our dinner-parties, and looking after our pet ocelots while we go on holiday.

"But ye gods, the price one pays for these small services! Take one's eye off him for an instant and he's poured himself a generous measure of one's best Scotch, and sprawled himself out at his ease in one's favourite armchair with the evening paper.

"Like as not he's also taken his shoes off to aerate his feet. Moreover, he hums to himself endlessly, with a strange, infuriating *shushing* noise, which I believe is supposed to represent the sound of a symphony orchestra. We all make fun of him behind his back, of course. But somehow that no longer seems enough."

After a lead like this, I should think, the floodgates would open, and the Letters to the Editor column would be full of brutally candid letters from everyone in the family.

"Sir,—May we say how heartily many of us ordinary aunts and uncles agree with your correspondent's remarks about our nephew? It is high time that the conspiracy of silence about his personal habits was broken.—Yours, etc., Arthur Wroxby, Millicent Wroxby, Clara Frayn Steadfast."

"Sir,—I regret to add to the melancholy tale of my cousin's shortcomings, but I have been present on at least two occasions when he has told deliberate untruths. Indeed, I have often been struck by his inability to look one straight in the eye. I wonder if this is an experience which has been shared by any other of your readers?—J. N. G. Portly-Walker, Godalming."

"Sir,—Your readers may be interested to know that Michael's indifferent social behaviour was the despair of his parents from an early age. But many of us in the family felt that they had only themselves to blame. They should have been much stricter with the boy, as I myself told them on more than one occasion, though small thanks I got for it. If only they could have foreseen what their thoughtless indulgence would lead to!—I am, &c., (Mrs.) Louisa Ironmaster, Southsea."

"Sir,—When he comes to our house, our granfather wissles through his teeth and makes boreing jokes which bore me and my brotheres and sisteres. He is a tall man, but boreing to have as a granfather.—(Miss) Phillida Frayn (aged 4)."

"Sir,—I was interested to see Mr. Portly-Walker's reference to my cousin's dishonesty. I am myself only a second cousin once removed, but on the few occasions we have met, Mr. Frayn has invariably breathed into my face and attempted to borrow money, saying that he has left his change in his other trousers, or got to the bank too late. It is high time that this man was hounded out of private life.—Yours faithfully, T. Wesley Topples, Stroud."

I don't like it, men—I don't like it one little bit. Let's stick with those grand old Interdepartmental Committees after all.

On The Receiving End

I see ... I see ... Yes, yes ... I see ...
Oh, really ...? Is that so ...?
I see ... I *see* ...! Good Lord ...! Good God ...!
No ...! Heavens ...! Really ...? *No* ...!

You *didn't* ...! Did you ...? How fantastic ...!
Of course ... Oh, naturally ...
Fantastic ...! No ...! Incredible ...!
An *albatross* ...! Blow me ...!

This is an extract from my long poem, "The Rime of the
Wedding-Guest." My intention is that it should be recited, or
rather murmured, simultaneously with the recitation of "The
Rime of the Ancient Mariner," as a sort of accompanying
ostinato.

The position of the man who tells a story has been very fully
explored in literature, of course—but the role and problems of
the person who has a story told to him have scarcely been
touched upon. It's not as easy as it looks to be on the receiving
end. One has to find ways of expressing one's continued
interest and comprehension—whether sincerely or not—
without interrupting the flow, and yet without seeming to have
passed into a state of trance, or of mindless repetitive grunting.

Where do you look, for a start? The narrator's eyes seem the
logical place. But which eye—the left or the right? And can one
stand gazing at either of them for more than a few seconds at a
time?

A psychologist called Michael Argyle has been doing some
experiments on this sort of problem at Oxford. The farther
away his subjects sat from their interlocutor, he found, the
more they kept their eyes on the interlocutor's eyes during the
conversation. The closer the subjects sat, the more they tended
to avoid the interlocutor's eyes (I suspect because of this
difficulty of deciding which eye to choose at close range).

The optimum distance turned out to be between four and six feet.

But even at this distance the subjects were noticeably disconcerted when the interlocutor's eyes were concealed behind dark glasses; and more disconcerted still when the eyes were visible but the rest of the interlocutor was hidden.

The Ancient Mariner, of course, was partially concealed behind a long grey beard, from the midst of which he held the Wedding-Guest with his glittering eye. He also held him with his skinny hand, which suggests an eyeball-to-eyeball distance of two feet or less. The whole situation for the Wedding-Guest, on Argyle's showing, can scarcely have been more disturbing. No wonder that he left afterwards like one that hath been stunn'd, and that a sadder and a wiser man he rose the morrow morn.

And while one shifts one's gaze uneasily about between right eye, left eye, and Adam's apple, one hears the sort of depressing subarticulate noise issuing involuntarily from one's lips which occupies the Wedding-Guest in my poem from stanza 57 to stanza 79 inclusive. Thus:—

Um, um . . . um, um . . . yep, yep . . . um, um . . .
Aha . . . uh-huh . . . ah . . . oh . . . ?
Sure . . . quite . . . uh-huh . . . yep, yep . . . yop, yop . . .
Yup, yup . . . aha . . . oho . . .

And one nods. Or I nod. I can't stop myself—there seems to be some direct link between my eardrums and my nodding muscles.

I find myself nodding even when I'm only one among an audience of many. Lecturers catch sight of me, nodding away in apparently eager agreement with every point they make, and they gradually get round to delivering the lecture exclusively to me, unmindful of my surreptitious attempts to seize hold of my head and keep it still.

But it's worse to be an audience of one among one, as on guided tours of remote caves and castles on rainy days in late September. When I was an undergraduate I attended a course of lectures with an audience which dwindled swiftly as the weeks went by from six to one. The one was me, and I couldn't dwindle any further because the lecturer was my supervisor, which encouraged him to take the liberty of calling to collect me on his way to the lecture-room.

They were nine o'clock lectures, and on several occasions I was in bed when he arrived. He would wait politely while I got up and got dressed. Then we would walk to the lecture-room together, and I would sit down somewhere around row three, while he leant over the lectern and delivered at me the lecture he had always given at nine o'clock on that particular Wednesday of the Michaelmas term ever since he had first written it as a young graduate in 1915 or so.

If I so much as blew my nose or glanced out of the window, of course, he'd lost his entire audience. It was a fearful responsibility. I thought several times that I'd have nodded my head right off on to the floor by ten o'clock.

One feels an overwhelming need in this sort of situation to vary the nodding and grunting with a few intelligent questions. One of the reasons the Wedding-Guest has such a glazed look in my poem from stanzas 13 to 21 is that he's working out some keen questions for stanza 22, which goes:—

> What was the tonnage of this ship?
> For what port was she bound?
> And was she gimbel-rigged, or gyved?
> And were her gaskets sound?

Then he's looking glazed again from stanzas 72 to 79 because he's thinking, My God, it's 50 stanzas now since I last made an articulate remark of any sort! I must tell the old boy some anecdote about myself, to show how much I sympathise. So in stanza 80 he suddenly compresses his lips and looks into the distance and says:—

> It's odd, you know, your saying this,
> Because when I was staying
> At Brightlingsea I hired a boat . . .
> —I'm sorry, you were saying . . . ?

Because the old bloke is just sweeping on regardless—and getting all the credit from the critics.

Take my advice: Don't wait to be told—get telling first.

A Hand of Cards

Bernard—

> *With All Good Wishes*
> *for a Merry Christmas*
> *and a Happy New Year!*

> —from Charles (Edwards!)

I don't know whether you remember me—we used to prop up the bar of the Rose and Crown together occasionally in the good old days, in dear old London town. How are you keeping back there in England, you old reprobate? Look me up if you're ever passing through New Zealand.

*

Bernard and Jean—

> *Wishing You a Very*
> *Merry Christmas and the*
> *Happiest of New Years*

> —from Charles

Congratulations on your marriage—saw it in the *Times* airmail edition. Nice work if you can get it. Meant to write on the spot. Anyway, cheers to you both.

*

Bernard, Jean, and Baby Flora (!)—

> *All Best Wishes for*
> *Xmas and the New Year*

> —from Charles and Kitty (!)

Charles took the plunge at last, as you can see! Many congrats on the Flora effort—saw it in the *Times*—meant to write. You must come out and see us some time.

Bernard, Jean, Flora, and Polly (!)—

> *To Wish You a*
> *Joyous Christmas*

> —from Charles, Kitty, Gareth (!),
> and Luke (!!)

Yes, you did hear right—twins! Identical—fair, with Charles's nose and mouth. Born 14 July—same day as Fall of Bastille! Charles had to be revived with brandy. Gareth ate ear-ring last month, otherwise everything OK. Tremendous congrats on Polly—meant to write.

*

Jean, Flora and Polly—

> *The mail coach dashes thru' the snowy ways*
> *To bring good cheer and news of happy days!*

> —from Charles, Kitty, Gareth,
> Luke, Lionel (!), and Mother.

Dreadfully sorry about you and Bernard, but I'm sure you're usually better off apart in these cases. Great shock when we got your last year's card, meant to write at once, but you know how it is, particularly with Lionel and all the rest of it. Lionel was a slight mistake, of course! Mother's moved in to help out.

*

Bernard, Jean, Flora, Polly, and Daisy (!)—

> *Peace on Earth, Goodwill to Men*

> —from Kitty and Walter
> (CRAIGIE!), not to mention
> Gareth, Luke, Lionel, Mother,
> Victoria and Georgina!

Heartiest congrats on you and Bernard getting together again—further hearty congrats on weighing in so smartly with Daisy! Meant to write as soon as your last Xmas card arrived. Walter and I were married in Auckland on 9 June, reception for 120, two days' honeymoon at Rotorua while mother looked after children. Victoria and Georgina are Walter's children by first marriage, of course (!) Walter is engineer—low temperature. Poor Charles is coming over to England in New Year, told him to look you up.

*

Bernard, Jean, Flora, Polly, Daisy, and James (!)—

> *Hearty Good Wishes for*
> *a Merry Xmas and a*
> *Prosperous New Year!*

> —from Kitty, Walter, Gareth, Luke, Lionel, Mother, Victoria, Georgina, Murray, Lester and Baby Linda.

Congrats on James—my word you keep at it! Victoria and Georgina had lovely joint wedding at St Margaret's, Wanganui, in Feb. Vicky married Murray West (his father's in agricultural machinery down near Christchurch), Georgie married Lester Dewie—nice young man, went to school in England (Thorpehurst—know it?), now learning hotel business. Georgie's baby Linda born (prematurely!) 3 Aug. Did poor Charles ever show up in GB?

*

Charles (!), Jean, Flora, Polly, Daisy, and James—

> *When the Yule log brightly burns*
> *And brings its Christmas cheer,*
> *To days gone by fond Mem'ry turns,*
> *And old friends far and near!*

> —from Kitty, Walter, Gareth, Luke, Lionel, Victoria, Murray, Georgina, Lester, Linda, Sukie, and Simon.

Heartiest congrats from all of us on you and Charles! V. best wishes—all tickled pink. Shameful of me not to write in summer when I heard news but Vicky was just producing

158

Simon, and then Georgie was having Sukie while I looked after Linda, then Mother passed quietly away.

*

Charles, Jean, Flora, Polly, Daisy, James, Dinah (!), Gareth, Luke, and Lionel—

> *Yuletide Greetings!*
>
>> —from Kitty, Walter, Victoria, Murray, Georgina, Lester, Linda, Sukie, Simon, and Gabriel.

Congratulations on Dinah! Don't know how you do it! Gabriel (Simon's brother) born 7 Oct. in flood. Hope Gareth, Luke, and Lionel are settling down all right with their father for Xmas, seems very quiet here without them, though Lester's mother is coming for Xmas Day (she's just lost her husband, sadly) plus his two sisters Charmian and Henrietta, so house will be quite full. Walter has ulcer.

*

Charles, Jean, Flora, Polly, Daisy, James, Dinah, Gareth, Luke, Lionel, Georgina, Lester, Linda, Sukie, and Jane—

> *Christmas Comes But Once a Year,*
> *and When it Comes it Brings Good Cheer!*
>
>> —from Kitty, Walter, Victoria, Murray, Simon, Gabriel, Nicholas, Charmian, Henrietta, *Bernard* (!), Cecilia and Timothy.

Hope the boys are enjoying their Xmas jaunt as usual and behaving themselves. So good of you to have Georgie and Lester and the girls for Xmas while they're over in England, hope Charles will be up and about again soon. Guess what, Bernard's here! Coming for Xmas Day with his new wife Cecilia and their baby Timothy (three months). Sends his love—says he doesn't send Xmas cards any more. I know what he means—once you start it never ends.

With All The Stops Out

"The crossings or hybridisations of the media," writes Marshall McLuhan in "Understanding Media," "release great new forces and energy as by fission or fusion." And he mentions a few of these dynamic "media mixes," as he calls them—sound films, for instance.

I think there's a new hybrid medium developing under our noses right now—and it's nothing less than a full-scale fusion of the old print culture and the new electric culture! It could be brighter than a thousand suns.

Take this piece of print, which comes from a manifesto (in favour of poetry designed for personal performance by its author) written by the American poet Charles Olson, and quoted by Bernard Bergonzi in the current *Encounter:*

"And the line comes (I swear it) from the breath, from the breathing of the man who writes, at the moment that he writes, and thus is, it is here that, the daily work, the W O R K gets in, for only he, the man who writes, can declare, at every moment, the line its metric and its ending—where its breathing shall come to, termination. . . ."

Recognise it? The sound of the human voice, as exactly transcribed into the print medium by way of an electric medium—recording!

Of course, we've been familiar with transcribed speech in interviews for a long time now, both in journalism ("Sir Harold Sidewinder talks to O. J. Sprout") and literature ("My Story," by ex-King Libido of Psychomania, as told to H. Spencer Upcreep). But I think this can now be seen as an intermediate form, which used the technology of the tape-recorder while attempting to preserve all the conventions of writing and the print culture. The authors always have their subjects talking in complete sentences, each with a beginning, a main verb and an end. They don't record repetitions, I-thinks or uncovenanted rhymes and alliterations at all. I'm not suggesting that they misreport—no doubt they actually *hear* the commas, semi-colons and fresh paragraphs. They probably hear the names correctly spelt, too.

But even highly educated and articulate people don't talk in this way; they talk like Mr. Olson writes. Professor Quirk demonstrated this very clearly in his work for the Communications Research Centre at University College back in the fifties. The transcripts which television and broadcasting companies make of programmes involving spontaneous comment and conversation have been proving it ever since.

In fact these transcripts, as one now sees, are the direct precursors of Olsonism—the unacknowledged expression of the age! I have one in front of me now, of a conversation involving myself. It's a breathtaking document—in some ways even more striking than the Olson piece. Some of the credit for this must, I think, go to me—my patterns of thought and expression seem to be uniquely convoluted, almost baroque in their structure. But the anonymous transcriber has done marvels—he's heard the spoken words afresh, as pure sound, the way the Impressionists saw light, or the Cubists form, and he's liberated himself from many of the conventions of punctuation and spelling which still shackle Mr. Olson.

Sprout: So you intend to work in this hybrid medium henceforth?

Oneself: Yes well the point is the fact is it is kind of a rediscovery of one's, I mean there is a kind of over-sophistication abroad today which, when we are trying to as it were rediscover our, well just take one aspect, isn't it rather misleading to represent all sentences as having ends because in real life you tend to find more the sort of sentences in which you get to the middle of which and then when you've got there having started off in one way you find in the middle that the beginning. . . .

Sprout: Exactly.

Oneself: I mean that the beginning of which when you've got to the middle. . . .

Sprout: Quite.

Oneself: And then again I mean you know you start out on a sentence with perhaps I as the subject and before one knows where one is we find that one's not I but you. I mean you don't know from one moment to the next whether one's me or you,

which is life all over. And it's not just me and you, you find
yourself referring to Dusty Yevsky perhaps or Ian S. Coe and a
whole Pantheon of names who've never been so much as
mentioned in print before, well a whole new world is opened
up.
Sprout: But have we gone far enough?
Yourself: No we must obviously do away with commas and so
on altogether and put in the *ers* and *ums* instead because *er*
when you come to think about it *er* these are the true punctuation signs of ordinary speech *um* and of course one would need
to indicate circling gestures chopping motions raisings of the
eyebrows lickings of the lips thoughtful intakes of breath
etcetera.
Sprout: I find this *er* extraordinarily *aaaaah* interesting
Myself: And I mean you know one really ought to try doing
without gaps between the words because they really are something purelyvisual *er* notaudibleatall
Sprout: Thisismostexciting
Ourself: And of course one one one one one thinks as one goes
along anyway I've tried to show the whole thing in a novel I'm
writing now which starts

   Chapterone *er* Oneday no Onefineday *um* inthecityofofofof
er I'llthinkofthenameinamoment *er* livedamancalled Arthur-
Brown ohLordno JamesMaltravers nono WalterWavertree
ohGodforbid *um* (hand passes despairingly across brow)
Nolet'sbeginagain *er* Onefineday

Child and Superchild

It's terrible to think of the manpower the world has wasted up
to now by failing to commence the education of the young in
earliest infancy. Children have been allowed just to throw
away the first five years of their lives; when all the time they
could—as researchers, journalists and anxious parents all over
the world are now coming to realise—have been learning to get
ahead and lay the foundations of successful careers.

Now all that's a thing of the past. These days, the mother who has her child's future at heart sets to work before it's even born, and spends part of each day during pregnancy inside a decompression suit to increase the supply of oxygen to its brain, with the result that it subsequently learns to crawl and walk (and presumably also to graduate and get a peerage) earlier than less fortunate children from underdecompressed homes.

The privileged infant has not long opened its eyes upon the world, of course, before its loving mother is holding up Teach Your Baby to Read cards in front of it, and developing its "need for achievement" (the *n* Ach rating, as identified by Professor McClelland of Harvard) by setting "moderately high achievement goals" and helping the child to reach them in a "warm, encouraging and non-authoritarian" way.

And now, I see from the series of articles on "Success before Six" in the *Sunday Times*, it's been discovered that parents have "a potent chance to accelerate the intellectual development of their children" by the way they talk to them. The helpful parent should speak to his child in a rich vocabulary, using "modelled" conversation techniques rather than "systematic expansion," and an "elaborated code" rather than a "restricted" one.

According to a book called "Educating Your Baby" which is quoted in the series, "a parent can help the child by repeating consonant and vowel sounds, slowly and deliberately . . . by letting the baby see lip movements, and pausing to let him imitate them. One compresses the lips into a thin line and parts them with the sound, 'ba'. Smiling at the baby may induce him to smile in return; lips parting then produces the syllable and mother and child laugh gleefully. The syllable can be made repeatedly; 'ba-ba-ba' until the child is ready for something else."

The next part of the training course, according to the article, is the Naming of Parts. "If this is started early enough then by the time he is 12 months old he will be able to point to parts of his body when asked. 'Can you touch your mouth? Touch your mouth.' Show him how. 'Good boy. You're touching your mouth.' (*Not*: 'You are doing it.')"

Certainly not! With that kind of teaching he could fail his

one-plus! Anyway, from the age of 18 months the object is to get the child to repeat after his mother or father the names of familiar objects. Then we get on to the more severe disciplines involved in advanced studies.

"Once the child can talk," says the article, "it is best to ask for complete responses to questions. 'How many days are there in a week, Alice?' 'Seven.' 'Good. But it could be better. The correct answer is "There are seven days in a week." Say for me, "There are seven days in a week." ' "

It sounds to me as if they're having trouble with this Alice child. Isn't this casual, slipshod approach to academic work, this lackadaisical mumble of "Seven," only too typical of youth today? I bet Alice has a sugar cigarette hanging out of the corner of her mouth during lectures—I bet she tries to cut compulsory hopscotch! The next thing you know, she'll be sprawling on the floor with a banner outside her father's study, demanding another threepence a week pocket money and a bigger say in planning her syllabus.

Where did Alice's parents go wrong? Was the pressure in her mother's decompression suit not low enough? Did her father hurry her on to "dad-dad-dad" before she'd fully mastered "ba-ba-ba"? In any case, she's sadly retarded in her development compared with Algernon, a child of my acquaintance whose intellectual life was accelerated in accordance with *really* modern methods.

In the first place, Algernon's parents took care to conceive him during the first hour of his mother's fertile period, in accordance with a survey by Progel and Hergstrom which showed that early-fertilised ova have the highest chance of A/B class membership in later life.

Next, his parents began talking formatively to him by the use of deep-penetration sonic waves while he was still in the womb. By the time he was born he could recite the subjunctive of most irregular French verbs reasonably reliably, and his parents felt free to address him thenceforth, as they croodled encouragingly over his cot, entirely in mathematical equations, to which the delighted infant would reply by gurgling the solutions, with many a gleeful laugh.

He spent a year travelling to broaden his horizons after leaving school, and therefore did not go up to Cambridge until he was nearly four. He took his Ph.D. at six, after two very fruitful months at M.I.T., and entered the Mashmaestro Corporation on the research side, where he enjoyed a brilliant career, rising to become head of his department at the age of seven, and joining the Board in the following year.

And there he will remain for the next 57 years. His hobbies are conkers and marbles, and he is writing what is likely to be the standard work on the after-effects of precocity, entitled "The Problems of Teenage Senility."

Get older younger, that's the aim, and come fresh and unspoiled to second childhood.

In the Morris Manner

Two very different styles of life are defined by the two styles of architecture which seem most pervasively influential in our time—the austere classicism of Mies van der Rohe and his followers on the one hand, and the currently more fashionable informality of Charles and Ray Eames on the other.

It's not easy to know which to aspire to. So I think it's worth saying that there is a *third* lifestyle, fundamentally different again, which has been developed over the years by our friends Horace and Doris Morris and indeed our good selves. All we lack at the moment is an architecture to put around it.

In the Miesian canon, if I understand it, the overriding goal is perfection of form. The skin of the building is the most formally perfect solution possible of its function, expressed (usually) in terms of glass to keep the weather out and steel to hold up the glass. The contents are as important to the form of the whole as the transparent skin; so they, too—furniture, carpets, pictures, the lot—are as strictly located by the architect as the drains.

An architect friend of mine who recently visited the famous Glass House that Philip Johnson, Mies's associate, built for himself in Connecticut reports that discreet marks are placed on the carpet, when new staff are engaged, to show exactly where each chair is to stand.

I see the attractions: four days out of seven I should like nothing better than to have an authoritarian architect design my life for me. But then I see the attractions of the opposite conception, too, as developed out of the Mies tradition by Mr. and Mrs. Eames, and enshrined in the house they have built for themselves at Santa Monica, in California.

According to Geoffrey Holroyd, in an issue of *Architectural Design* devoted to the Eameses recently, "the house is filled with a huge collection of toys—objects of indigenous Santa Fé folk culture, tumbleweed, driftwood, desert finds of great variety—placed everywhere ... Mies wants all glass and no clutter; Eames wants clutter, 'functioning decoration.'" The house is also full of Eames chairs—"the first chairs," according to another contributor, "which can be put into any position in an empty room."

This bald description makes the Eames life-style sound superficially rather similar to Horace and Doris Morris's and our own. The concept of *clutter* is certainly very central to our thinking. Our houses contain huge collections of toys, mostly broken, together with a random precipitation of pieces of wood, pebbles, old tin cans and cardboard boxes, broken chalk, dolls' legs, scattered heads, empty bottles, and torn envelopes with examples of indigenous child-art on the back. Our chairs, too, are arranged all kind of anyhow.

But a glance at photographs of the interior of the Eameses' house shows that their clutter is clutter only in the loosest sense; it's not clutter in the strict sense that we and Horace and Doris Morris mean at all. The Eameses' tumbleweed has tumbled neatly on to rows of hooks on the wall. The driftwood has drifted into an elegant complex just outside the garden door. The objects of indigenous Santa Fé folk culture have arranged themselves on a square board squared off with a square table, and the chairs have rained down from heaven into positions of the most geometrical exactitude.

The general appearance, in fact, places Charles and Ray Eames pretty firmly in the tradition of our good friends Christopher and Lavinia Crumble, whose extensive collection of folk-junk and *objets achetés* has also arranged itself about the living-room with an effortless casual elegance which is entirely alien to the Horace and Doris Morris style.

A completely different approach to the organic development of the clutter is involved. When Christopher Crumble finishes reading a book, for instance, and tosses it casually down on the coffee-table, it lands squarely on top of "Giovanni Battista Piranesi and the Origins of Op Art" (Limburger & Brie. 7 gn.), the edges parallel, the diagonal extending the diagonal of the alabaster lamp-base standing at the golden section of the table. When Horace Morris or I toss a book down, however, it behaves in a much more radically casual fashion. It hits an abandoned Wellington boot standing in an empty soup bowl, perhaps, loses its jacket, and comes down half-open, halfway into an ashtray which is teetering half off the table and half on, kept in balance only by being half covered with a pair of old trousers which have been put out for mending.

Later, one throws down the daily paper, half-open, on top of the ashtray, the book, the boot, the trousers, and all the rest of it, whereupon half the paper slides down the side of the heap, and wafts away to fetch up along with the book jacket, half under the sofa and half out.

One's wife comes tramping through the broken chalks, pebbles, and amputated dolls' legs, carrying a large cardboard box marked Heinz Spaghetti with Tomato Sauce, and full of old bills and grey woollen socks. With unthinking deftness she half folds up the half-open newspaper to half make room for it, so that the box forms, some days later, an attractively unstable podium on which to rest the load of old colour supplements which have finally slipped off the top of the television set.

Within a week or two one is hacking one's way back down to table level again, hefting the sliding sea of colour supplements up by the armful, and dumping them into a Sainsbury's Australian Pear Halves box, which one shoves into the kitchen while one tries to think what the hell has happened to a Wellington boot and a book which have mysteriously gone missing. And didn't one have a spare pair of trousers at one stage of one's career . . . ?

It's a style of life all right. All we need is a style of architecture that makes sense of it.

Pas Devant les Enfants

It's not television which is the greatest threat to the art of conversation, in my experience; it's children.

The Victorians were certainly 100 years ahead of their time on this problem, with their doctrine of children being seen and not heard. If the children are heard then any adults present are not; and the Victorians, with their usual sensitive concern for parent-care, realised that the most frightful psychic damage could be inflicted upon adults whose natural drive to communication and self-expression was persistently frustrated.

What I don't quite understand, though, is the Victorians' inexplicable permissiveness in letting children be *seen*. A child, at any rate a small child, doesn't need to be heard to disrupt all rational intercourse in the vicinity; its visible presence is quite enough.

A child is rather like a television set, in fact—and turning the sound down when company comes isn't enough to prevent all eyes in the room from being irresistibly drawn towards it. How often has one seen a whole roomful of normally articulate adults sitting bemused around their assembled offspring, bereft of all powers of speech, apart from the sort of desultory facetious comment which is usually reserved for the Westerns? And television sets have the great advantage that they can be switched off.

Of course, if children are disruptive with the sound turned down, they're worse still when it's turned up. Sound and vision tend to be deployed to their fullest communication-destroying effect just when a matter of some delicacy and importance has to be conveyed between husband and wife. Just when Mr. Ricardo was trying to explain to Mrs. Ricardo about Marginal Utility—that's when the children would have switched on the jammers: just when the Tsar and Tsarina were discussing whether to invade Poland next season.

Or take the afternoon that Pythagoras came out of his study looking rather pleased with himself.

"You know this work I've been doing recently on hypotenuses?" he says to his wife, trying to sound casual. "Well, a rather interesting point struck me this afternoon—I don't know whether you think it sounds reasonable—that the *square* on the hypotenuse must be equal to...."

But at this point a ringing cry from the lavatory interrupts the exposition.

"Will you wipe my b-o-o-o-t-tom!"

"Sorry," says his wife when she gets back. "What were you saying? Something about hypotenuses."

"I was just going to say that the square on the hypotenuse...."

"Mummy!"

"Sh, Jemima! Daddy's talking."

"... that the square on the hypotenuse is equal to...."

"But, *Mummy* ...!"

"*Sh*, Jemima! You mustn't interrupt when someone's speaking! How many times have I had to tell you?"

"... equal to the sum of the squares on the other two sides!"

"I see. Now, what's the trouble, Jemima?"

"James is being horrible to me! He's taken my zoetrope!"

"James, give Jemima back her zoetrope at once! Sorry, Py. What were you saying?"

"I said it."

"All hypotenuses are equal...?"

"God give me strength! Why do you *never* listen to what I say? I said the square on the hypotenuse is equal to the sum...."

"The what?"

"The *sum* ... the SUM ...! My God. I can't hear myself speak! Will you SHUT UP, you two! If I hear one more word out of either of you, I'll throw that damned zoetrope into the Aegean, and that'll be the end of it! Now, the *square* on the *hypotenuse*...."

"Yes, yes, I got that bit.... Just a moment—James, what *have* you been doing to your face....? Well, go and wash it off at once.... Sorry—'the square on the hypotenuse'—I am listening.... Don't just rub it on your sleeve, James....!

Sorry, Py, but if he's left to go wandering round in that condition there'll be shaving cream all over the house.... Anyway, the square on the hypotenuse...."

"Will you wipe my b-o-o-o-o-t-tom!"

It's Pythagoras's turn this time. "Where were we?" he asks wearily when he returns. "Oh, yes, the square on the hypotenuse. Well, all I was going to say was that it's equal to the sum of the squares.... *Now* what are you doing? What the hell do you keep turning round for?"

"Sorry—I was just trying to see why Jemima was so quiet all of a sudden."

"Oh, for God's sake!"

"Go on about the square on the hypotenuse."

"It was nothing."

"Don't be silly."

"It wasn't of the slightest importance.... Well, I was merely going to say that it was equal to the sum of the squares on the other two sides. That's all."

"But, Py, that's absolutely *fascinating!* I'd never have guessed it! Marvellous ...! What *is* Jemima up to, by the way? Is she sulking? Can you see? She's not sucking her thumb, is she?"

"Yes. ... No.... I don't know! She's not there.... Look, are you interested in my work on the hypotenuse or aren't you?"

"Of course I am. I think it's tremendously important.... I'd better just make sure she hasn't wandered out into the street...."

"I mean, I don't care whether you are or not. I just thought you *were*, that's all. It's just that once upon a time you used to *ask* me...."

"Will you wipe my b-o-o-o-o-t-tom!"

It's the trailing clouds of glory which Wordsworth observed hanging about children—that's what really disrupts communication. Glorious-looking clouds, certainly; but when you're in amongst them, like most clouds, pretty well indistinguishable from dense fog.

.

A Princess in Disguise

I believe society women are becoming more ambitious and serious-minded. In an earlier century they all wanted to take up careers as shepherdesses—now they want to become actresses. I put it down to education and female suffrage. Ex-Queen Soraya of Iran shot to stardom in the film industry recently. Now Lee Bouvier—otherwise known as Princess Lee Radziwill, and sister of Jacqueline Kennedy—has fought her way to the top of the ladder, and crowned a dazzling career with her appearance on the world's television screens in "Laura."

A hard struggle it was, as recounted in the *TV Times* last week. The first thing she did was to take some lessons in acting. She didn't just rush out and book six half-hours with the local elocution and tap-dancing teacher, of course; you can't take short cuts in this business. What she did was, "she mentioned her ambition to Alan Lerner [author of the musical 'My Fair Lady']; he mentioned it to an impresario, who recommended a coach to give her private drama lessons."

Her studies completed, she made her modest début on the stage—playing the lead in "The Philadelphia Story" in Chicago. After this rich and varied experience in the provinces she was ready to tackle anything. ". . . Her friend Truman Capote went to David Susskind and suggested putting her in a TV production. Capote . . . offered to write the script. He turned in the adaptation of 'Laura.'"

One can only wonder what the next step will be. Lucia di Lammermoor? Giselle? Or is her song and dance a little rusty? She told the *TV Times* that it was difficult to find good directors to work with. I suppose all the talented young millionaires and aristocrats one sees around simply don't have the dedication and stamina it takes. They only have to think of giving up every Thursday evening for a month and serving a week's apprenticeship in Glasgow or St. Louis, and their hearts fail them.

What I like is the very chivalrous and helpful part played by Mr. Lerner and Mr. Capote in Miss Bouvier's success story. Real knights in shining armour. Well, that's the way we writers are. Take my friend Ken Nocker and myself. We're besieged with requests from great ladies who want us to write verse-dramas for them, or get them parts in "The Avengers," and we always do our best to oblige.

Did you see ex-Queen Beatrice of Savoy in that play of Ken's at the Victoria Theatre, Screwe, recently? Ken rang me up in great excitement the day he discovered her.

"What a find!" he shouted. "She has a first-class figure, wonderfully expressive eyes, and very substantial holdings in De Beers and blue chip industrials."

"Yes, but can she act?" I queried keenly.

"Can she act?" he cried. "*Can she act?* Listen, that gracious lady is twelfth in succession to the throne of Romania, and a second cousin by marriage to the Duke of Kent! Anyway, she wants me to write a kind of light-hearted black comedy, with a part for her as a golden-hearted whore. A *kooky* golden-hearted whore, to be precise."

"Aren't kooky golden-hearted whores a little *passé*, at the moment?"

"Well, that's what she wants to play. Either that or Lady Macbeth, and I felt at this stage of her career . . . you know. . . . Anyway, I shall have a completely free hand. Her only con-dition is that she isn't asked to do anything undignified or unbecoming, and that her skirt comes down to the knee."

"She's not going to be standing on her dignity all the time, is she?"

"No, that's the wonderful thing about her! She just wants to start right at the bottom of the top, and be treated exactly like any other beginner. Of course, I'll have to see that each charac-ter calls her 'Your Majesty' on entering."

"Oh, of course."

"But thereafter it's just plain 'Ma'am.' In fact, I was thinking of making her not so much a golden-hearted whore as a golden-hearted madam. That would make it sound more natural, I think. It's very important that the other characters behave absolutely naturally with her, just as if they really were in a brothel—so long as they don't speak until she's spoken first."

Well, it all went off very well. Sir John Gielgud injured his back—he tripped over the footlights and fell into the orchestra pit while walking backwards out of the brothel bowing—but apart from that it was all very enjoyable, and surprisingly audible. In the front stalls, at any rate.

Of course, it's not just acting ambitions that Ken Nocker and I try to fulfil. Some of our rich friends want to be architects, or airline pilots. There was the lovely Lady Dimity Mincing, who couldn't rest until she had appeared as a barrister at the Old Bailey, and defended some innocent person wrongfully charged with a serious offence. We managed to pull strings and fix it for her, and it gave her a great sense of personal fulfilment; though I think she was a little disappointed with the verdict.

Our greatest triumph was arranging for Mrs. Jefferson T. Doppelganger III to fly over and perform a heart transplant at Guy's, before an invited audience. Of course, we insisted that she did a Red Cross first-aid course beforehand.

Anyway, *our* secret ambition is that some of our good friends will be able to repay our little kindnesses, and arrange with the millionaires of their acquaintance for us to have a go at being rich.

Facing the Music

In theory, television ought to be bringing the arts within reach (as they say) of millions who would not otherwise etc. etc. It seems reasonable enough. You've got sound, you've got vision. What more do you want to communicate every known art form, except perhaps gastronomy?

But in practice it doesn't work out too well. The sight of a great painting reproduced a foot high, in monochrome and in low definition, isn't a very compelling aesthetic experience. Nor is watching someone read poetry off the teleprompter— even a teleprompter with hand-tooled calf binding.

You'd think that the performing arts at least would be naturals. And, indeed, stage plays and opera are; but ballet is hopeless, and music is very tricky.

Most of the older arts have to be communicated on television, if at all, by suggestion and association. Details from paintings can be very poignant, glimpsed as the raw material for some quiz programme. Poetry can be highly effective, read as the background to film shots which are evocative in their own right. It's a sort of titillation, like the suggestion of sexual feeling by glimpses of suspenders; it's not really art itself which is being communicated, but a kind of nostalgia for art experiences with which one is already familiar.

Music is the most tantalising of all. It's odd; surely the performers (the perfect monochrome subject in their black tail-coats and white ties) are no smaller or less distinct on a television screen than they would be from the back of a concert hall?

But there's something about the sight of them which unsettles television producers, at any rate, and makes them feel the medium's being misused. They tried to get round it first of all by creative cross-cutting. They'd cut to the oboes to show them playing five particularly significant notes. Dissolve to horns, for a telling tootle from them. Then they'd show you the piano keyboard superimposed over the clarinets, so you'd know that the piano and the clarinets were playing significant bits simultaneously. If only they'd put up sub-titles, too, saying "coda," or "modulation into E flat," or "attribution of this passage doubtful," we'd really have known where we stood.

Evidently the producers still weren't happy, though, because the tendency is increasingly to show music only in some secondary role, as the by-product of its performers' personalities, or as the raw material of more telegenic processes.

Instead of actual performances we are shown rehearsals. A little music occurs—then some celebrated and well-loved character in the musical world waves his arms despairingly and stops everyone. "No, no, no, no!" he cries in compellingly broken English. "Not *so*—la, la-la, la—like from leetle mouses who are frighten of cat. Beeg beeg! *LA, LA-LA, LA....!"*

And again music breaks out; but of course by this time we are all turning to each other at home and saying, "My God, what a tyrant! But they all *love* him, you know—he's such a character!"

Or they show the musicians in question on tour. We see them starting Opus 59 No. 1 at a concert in Denver, but after a few bars they leave the music playing of its own accord on the sound-track, slip into sports shirts and drive by a scenic route through the Rockies to some millionaire's ranch, where the cellist falls amusingly into the swimming-pool. By the time he's out, and had a drink, and complications have set in on the Beethoven, they've abandoned it anyway, and started playing the second Bartok quartet in Salt Lake City.

The latest and most fruitful technique is to show the music being recorded for stereo, a complex process which gives scope for every conceivable sort of human and technical diversion—and even offers a legitimate excuse for superimposing more entertaining sounds over the music while it's actually being played, in the form of the "talkback" between the recording engineers.

"Stand by for the drum roll.... Fade up Don Ottavio and stand by to kill Miss Nielsen as soon as she's finished her A.... We're getting a bit of resonance off Siegfried's glasses, aren't we, George....?"

Fascinating, certainly. In fact, when you come to think about it, a lot of television itself isn't all that televisual; it might be greatly improved by the application of the same sort of techniques. A man sitting reading the news out, for instance—wouldn't it be much more exciting, much more real, to have the *rehearsal* of it, with all the talk-back between control room and studio floor audible?

"... five, four, three, two, one—cue Bob." *"The Prime Minister told the House of Commons today that...."* "Hold it there! Something's wrong with Bob's microphone.... Well, get him to sit a bit closer, then.... All right? All right—from the top, everyone.... five, four, three, two, one—cue Bob."

"The Prime Minister told the House of Commons today that...." "Hold it, everyone! The lines on Bob's forehead are strobing."

And if a programme about the engineers recording the music is better than just the music, surely it's logical to suppose that a programme about the cameramen filming the engineers recording the music would be better still, and that even better than *that* would be a programme about the cameramen filming the cameramen filming etc. etc. Lord, think of the richness of the talkback!

"Go right in tight, two!" "Back a bit, one! No, my God, Ken's two's right behind you!" "Get that blasted mike up out of the picture!" "Come back down with Miss Sutherland's mike, damn you!" "Up a bit, three!" "Down a shade, three!" "Track round on to Ken's one, two!" "In on to Dick's two, one....!"

It may be slightly spoiled by interference from various hooligans singing and otherwise creating a disturbance in the background. But it should prove once and for all that it's possible to get television across on television.

57 Types of Ambiguity

To the Pope and his advisers, the subject of contraception seems to be what power politics were to Shakespeare, or Nature was to the Romantics—an inexhaustible inspiration to the most profound and astonishing literary utterance.

Again and again, reading the works of the Papal school on the subject, one is struck by their universality, their fertile ambiguity, their articulation of feelings and experiences for which one has never before found words.

Take just for a start the minority report of the Pope's advisory commission. The Church's traditional position on contraception *must* be right, the four dissenting members are said to have argued, "because the Catholic Church ... could not have so wrongly erred during all these centuries of its history."

Heavens, but that touches a chord! I feel they've seen into my soul! In one sentence those good and holy men have captured the inmost logic of my attitude to politics, religion— indeed, contraception itself. They've cut through all the specious tangle of particular argument I might have used, and located the unacknowledged real one—that I've thought what I've thought about these subjects since the age of 16 or 17, and I just *can't* have been wrong for all those years.

Of course, a process does sometimes occur which, seen from the outside, might be described as changing one's mind. But somehow it doesn't feel like that inside. Indeed, what it does feel like was beyond the range of language until the Vatican Press officer got to work on it.

He was asked, according to George Armstrong, the Rome correspondent of the *Guardian*, to elucidate the Pope's statement last October—that while he needed more time to study the question of contraception, this didn't mean that the Church's teachings on the subject were "in a state of doubt."

"The teaching of the Church," explained the Press officer, "is now in a state of certainty. After the Pope completes his study of the matter, the Church will move from one state of certainty to another state of certainty."

Yes! That's how it is—that's exactly how it is! You're going along in a complete state of certainty about something—the ludicrousness of Victorian architecture, say, or the moral inferiority of television—and everyone you know thinks the same.

Then various public crackpots start saying the opposite. Victorian architecture ought to be preserved, they bleat; television culture involves the whole man in a way that the print culture does not. You enjoy a good laugh at their antics. Then some of the people you know start falling for the same nonsense themselves! It doesn't bring one's own views into any state of doubt, of course. But then one day one hears oneself talking about the subject—and one realises that somehow, quite unconsciously, one has completed one's study of the matter and moved without a break to another and indeed opposite state of certainty!

So multi-levelled and many-faceted does the Pope himself wax on the subject that no one can tell whether he is still in the first state of certainty, or whether he has already moved on to the second. All that's certain is that *something* is certain—"It is certain that," he wrote in his encyclical "On the development of peoples." But what? "It is certain that public authorities can intervene, within the limit of their competence, by favouring the availability of appropriate information and by adopting suitable measures. . . ."

Many people, including apparently the director-general of the United Nations Food and Agriculture Organisation, believe this means that the Governments of the overpopulated countries should start actually handing out the suitable means (though whether in this case the suitable means are the sort which are digested through the proper channels, or the sort which are inserted in the appropriate place, is another rich field for speculation).

But according to an unsigned article in the Vatican newspaper, *L'Osservatore Romano*, described by the paper as "authoritative," this understanding of the encyclical is entirely wrong. When the Pope talks of "suitable measures," the article argues, he means growing more food; when he says that the authorities should "favour the availability of appropriate information," he means that they "must inform the country of its population problem."

My personal interpretation—and here I follow Sprout and Trouncer—is that the encyclical is so rich in meaning that it means *both* these things. And yet . . . neither. Only somehow . . . more, much more.

For isn't what the Pope is stating here really the general and unalterable moral rules governing suitable measures of *every* sort, and the availability of appropriate information *whatever* its subject? However many states of certainty we move through, two great moral beacons will guide us: if ever the question arises of what one should do about the availability of appropriate information, the answer is plain—favour it! And if ever a suitable measure crosses one's path—adopt it!

If only the gentlemen who wrote the Bible had been able to rise to this level of universality, how much less open to carping criticism it would be today! Really, it would be worth re-writing it from page one:—

"In the beginning the Competent Authority took certain steps.

"And the resultant state of affairs was without form, and void; and an unavailability of the appropriate information was upon the face of the steps. And the Competent Authority studied the question.

"And the Competent Authority said, Let further measures be adopted: and further measures were adopted.

"And the Competent Authority saw the further measures, that they were suitable: and the Competent Authority divided the measures from the steps.

"And the Competent Authority called the measures one thing, and the steps he called another. And what with one thing and another it was the first move in the right direction...."

In the Superurbs

The suburbs are all right after all. They are not, as has been commonly supposed, deserts of boredom, conformity, competitiveness and wife-swapping. They are not a dreadul social aberration which will in time be mercifully blotted out by enlightened town-planning, and living in them is not spiritually or morally inferior to living in the centre of cities.

These, at any rate, are the general conclusions which are likely to be drawn from the study of one particular lower-middle-class suburb in New Jersey made by the American sociologist Herbert J. Gans, and reported in his book "The Levittowners." His findings are said to have been violently attacked by orthodox professional opinion in America; a sure sign that they will eventually be violently accepted.

I accept Mr. Gans's findings right now, ahead of the rush, and only wish I'd had the wit to find them first. For a long time now I've nursed the vague project of writing a guide-book to my native London suburbs. Like most guide-books, it would touch upon the geography, history, architecture, customs and economy of the region. Whenever I've mentioned it to people they've either laughed and said it could be devastating, or asked if the suburban joke wasn't a bit played out. The idea of actually *describing* the suburbs, without either laughing at them or moralising about them, evidently seems to most people about as far-fetched as mapping a plate of mashed potato.

One of the reasons why the suburbs are thought to be such hotbeds, or perhaps coldbeds, of boring conformity is that they boringly *fail* to conform to the tastes of intellectuals. So anyone with intellectual leanings leaves at the first opportunity. Somewhere in the centre of the city, of course, they run into other disaffected intellectuals fleeing from *their* suburbs, and settle down on the spot to set up a boring conformity of their own.

Of course, the boring conformity of the intellectual community doesn't seem like boring conformity to the intellectuals, any more than the boring conformity of the suburbs seems like boring conformity to the suburbanites; each, to its adherents, seems full of the most stimulating diversity.

Let us not forget Progel's First Law of Social Appearances, which states: "The homogeneity of a group seen from outside is in inverse proportion to its heterogeneity seen from within." Or as Samuel Crink (1721–1897) puts it: "Likeness is in the eye of the unlike; the like see nothing but their unlikeness."

All the same, if I had money invested in the future prosperity of the suburbs, I think I should at this point discreetly begin to withdraw it. When moderate people like you and me, and all the others who will eventually come round to Mr. Gans's ideas, start thinking that an institution is a good thing after all, its prime is past; nothing but stagnation and decay lie ahead.

Remember what we thought of Victorian architecture, until it started to become ripe for demolition? Remember what filthy things we thought steam-trains and steam-ships were, until just before the rise of the motor-car and the aeroplane? Now, of course, we know that it is the motor-car and the aeroplane which are ruining our countryside and destroying our character. We shall come round to them only when they invent the ... whatever it is that will mark the end of our civilisation next.

This is the general moral history of ideas: in their mewling infancy they are interesting and challenging and on the point of opening up a wonderful new age. Then, when they grow strong and effective, and start opening up the wonderful new age, it turns out that they are inhuman, soul-destroying, contemptible, and ridiculous. And finally, in old age, when their strength begins to fail, they are regarded with understanding and affection, and showered with honours.

Remember how television was turning us all into a nation of square-eyed morons until McLuhan said really it was doing us all a world of good and the young were growing up as a new electronic super-race? Immediately, of course, we hear that fewer and fewer young people are watching television.

The other day I heard an architect talking nostalgically about pre-fabs as the best attempt yet at popular housing. High-rise flats—created in a messianic attempt to avoid the suburban sprawl we now think might be fine after all, and currently reviled in their turn—even these we shall one day come to feel affection for. Truly, there is almost no limit to the capacity of human beings to adapt themselves to the ideas imposed upon them for their own good.

It's odd how we feel impelled to react to everything in moral terms. Why does *everything* have to seem good or bad to us? Particularly when we know that whatever we now think good we shall eventually think bad, and vice versa. We're like tossed pennies, that can register nothing but heads or tails! Good God, is there really no aspect of the universe that we don't feel compelled either to encourage or discourage with our little smiles and frowns?

Let us put ten minutes aside each day to practise feeling morally numb. The more things in the universe which we can contemplate with neither approbation nor disapprobation, the more moral energy we shall have left to concentrate on the things which really do need something done about them. Let our commonest moral reaction be a shrug, our commonest moral discourse "I dunno," and "Sawright Ispose."

Then, faced with new ideas like adolescent self-determination and the spread of unfamiliar intoxicants, we might learn to express our unease and fear just as plain unease and fear, and instead of leaping in to condemn and ridicule, just modestly shuffle from foot to foot, and lick our lips uneasily, and tremble.

From the moral point of view (if one can say this) it would be great improvement.

H & C

One of the rewards of reading Marshall McLuhan is that it enables me to make my friend Horace Morris feel uneasy about not having read it, just as in the past I've made him feel very insecure for not understanding commitment and alienation, and not knowing what charisma was, and thinking that pop music was a bad thing after all the rest of us had realised it was a good thing.

The way the dissemination of ideas works around our way is that first my good friend Christopher Crumble gets to hear about them, and makes me feel insecure. Then I catch up and make Horace Morris feel insecure. By the time Horace had discovered the meaning and omnipresence of charisma, for example, I was right off it—no one seemed charismatic to me any more, not even Harold Wilson or David Frost. I was on to "symbiosis"—and Christopher Crumble, the Speedy Gonzales of the intellect, was already out of "symbiosis" and into "I-Thou," or even "freakout."

What happens to ideas after Horace has cast them off I can't imagine. That far down in the market their secondhand value must have reached vanishing point.

Anyway, now it's McLuhan, and almost everything in the world, as I now realise, is *iconic*. Including McLuhan's own book, "Understanding Media." I've never come across anything more iconic, as I said to Horace.

"Iconic?" repeated Horace uneasily.

"Oh, tremendously iconic. I didn't know it was possible for a book to *be* so iconic. Have you read it, Horace?"

"Well, not exactly...."

"I think your lack of interest in books is very significant and interesting, Horace. Even without reading McLuhan you instinctively reject the print culture, and the whole repetitive, mechanical approach to life of which printing is the archetype. You realise that print means centralisation and uniformity. You're not satisfied with the shallow participation which is all books demand—the specialisation and fragmentation of human life which the print culture suggests."

"Well, you know, Michael..."

"You understand instinctively that print is a hot medium."

"Well...."

"You feel in your bones that this is the electric age—the age of the total involvement of the individual in humanity at large by way of television. You didn't need McLuhan to tell you that television was a cool medium—that it's low-definition, that it requires the participation of the viewer to give the image meaning. The truth is that you're a natural twentieth-century man, Horace!"

"Well, I watch a certain amount of television," he said uneasily. "But I must admit, I do read *some* books...."

"Oh, *some* books, sure. But how about medieval manuscripts, Horace? Do you read manuscripts at all?"

"Manuscripts? Oh God no, I certainly don't read manuscripts! I think I can truthfully claim that I've never read a single medieval manuscript in my life."

At this, of course, I became somewhat pensive.

"Oh," I said. "Oh. That's rather a pity. Manuscript is a cool medium."

"Well, of course, I've read a few modern...."

"Quite. How do you stand on strip cartoons, Horace? Do you look at the strip cartoons at all?"

He thought for some time, shifting uneasily about in his chair.

"N-o-o-o-o," he said at last. "No, I don't. I think I've always realised somehow that they were part of the print culture business—you know, very standardised and mechanical and...."

"I see. Well, *McLuhan* thinks strip cartoons are a cool medium. He may be wrong, of course."

"Oh, I wouldn't say that...."

"Do you listen to the radio at all, Horace?"

183

"Oh God yes! Oh God, I mean, I really feel that radio is an essential part of the electric culture...."

I was looking very grave indeed by this point in the interrogation, as you can imagine.

"Radio is a hot medium," I told him, as kindly as I could. "High definition. Involves visualisation. Caused the rise of Hitler, according to McLuhan. Still, no reason why you shouldn't enjoy it, if you want to. I suppose you like using the phone?"

"Oh God no!" said Horace hurriedly. "I mean, oh God yes! I mean no! Hate it! Can't stand all that visualisation, and so on...."

"Wrong again, I'm afraid, Horace," I said, shaking my head sadly. "The telephone's a cool medium. Low definition— involves participation. Still, you do watch television. That's something. What do you watch, Horace? 'Panorama'?"

'Yes—no! No, no, no, no! I watch things like—well—old movies."

"*Old movies*, Horace?"

"Bad old movies," he added hastily. But he could see from my expression that there was something wrong here. "I thought bad old movies were good?" he cried. "I thought bad old movies were the new thing?"

"My God, Horace!" I shouted, my tactful reserve breaking down at last. "Bad old movies were new three years ago! Bad old movies were back in the days of Susan Sontag! Listen, Horace, films are high-definition. Films don't involve the total participation of the viewer. Films are a relic of the mechanical print culture. Films are *hot*, Horace!"

So much for Horace Morris's pretensions to be cool electric man. Though after he'd had time to think about it, he said that he watched the old movies on BBC-2, with an inside aerial. Definition was so poor, he said, with three or four overlapping images and the picture going jump-jump-jump every minute, and viewer participation was so high, with the viewer springing up to shift the aerial back and forth round the room all the time, that the medium was cool enough to neutralise the heat of even the hottest film.

And when you consider that he's short-sighted, too.... Maybe he *is* cool electric man after all.

A Question of Character

Canon Montefiore's suggestion that Christ might have been a homosexual was bound to cause a stir; if only because many psychologists think that homosexuality is the result of having an inadequate father.

But it would still have caused offence, I think, if the Canon had speculated about Christ's heterosexual proclivities. Or, indeed, about the working of his digestion, or whether he had corns on his feet.

The truth is that there's not much you *can* say about Christ without its seeming inappropriate. There's even less you can say about God. "All-powerful," "eternal," "merciful," "just," and a number of other compliments are in order, but not, I feel, "shrewd," "charming," "keen," "cheerful," "tidy," "sporting," or "brave." In fact we've got in a rather odd tongue-tied state about our gods altogether, considering that the medieval schoolmen used to maintain that God had all possible attributes. That should have provided plenty to say about him.

Shrewd and charming he would of necessity be on this analysis. An inadequate father, of course—though this would be balanced out by his being a perfectly adequate father, too. He would also be hexagonal, Chinese, mother-fixated, 12 years old, soluble in dilute sulphuric acid, south-westerly veering to westerly, and entirely composed of blotting-paper soaked in minestrone.

Yet few people took the opportunity to describe him as such.

Other theologians maintained that he was the sum of all possible perfections, which would have reduced his range a good deal, but still left him with perfect conductivity, perfect insulation, 20/20 eyesight, and first-class honours in social anthropology.

But these characteristics were little remarked upon at the time.

And quite what's being asserted of God when it's said that he's merciful, etc., is difficult to know. Because if one queries whether God really is quite as merciful as he is cracked up to be, given the astonishing number of quite merciless things which occur under his jurisdiction, and which in any other organisation would lead to vociferous demands for his resignation, religious people are astonished at the naïvety of one's interpretation.

"Good heavens!" they cry, often laughing cheerfully as well. "When we say that God's merciful we don't mean that he's merciful in any merely human sense of the word! With our miserably limited understanding, and our pathetically inadequate language, we couldn't hope to make anything but the most incomplete and misleading attempt at describing him.

"There's no way of knowing what we mean when we say that he is merciful. For all we know, *God's* mercifulness may consist in just those very things which we, with our poor understanding, think of as merci*less*!"

Gods weren't always as indescribable as this. The Greeks didn't hesitate to characterise their team as lecherous meaning lecherous, jealous meaning jealous, and drunken meaning drunken. God is very clearly characterised by the Old Testament, too. He's the local dictator who invents his own laws as he goes along and insatiably demands flattery; the unsleeping father of his people and architect of their victories, who bullies his courtiers and plays cruel tricks on them, and who murders individuals and destroys whole communities who step out of line—a small-time Stalin, with something of Castro's showmanship.

Now that's what I *call* a god. Nobody could read the Old Testament without being stirred to wholesome indignation. But then the producers got worried about the series—felt it didn't reflect the changing tastes of the age, thought it might be having an anti-social influence. So they tried to make the chief character turn on goodness instead of sheer power. They stopped him murdering people, and had him helping them in distress instead.

A weaker piece of characterisation, in my opinion. And when people began to complain that the new character was implausible, and viewing figures dropped off, the producers made a disastrous series of concessions. Instead of strengthening the character again, they weakened him still further.

"All right," they said. "If people don't believe there could be this all-powerful magic character going round doing good deeds, let's have him *not* going round doing good deeds. Let's have him doing nothing—just being good, and feeling agonised by the awfulness of things, and trying to make everything all right in the end."

Down went the viewing figures again, naturally.

"No, listen, all right, we've got it now," said the producers desperately. "This is a kind of more subtle thing. When we say he's good, we don't mean he's good in any ordinary, obvious way. We mean he's got this secret code of his own which...."

And down went the figures once more.

"Hey, no, stop, we've rethought the whole product!" shouted the producers. "He's not a person at all! No, listen, you'll love this—he's a kind of scientific principle, a sort of abstract emotional kind of.... No, hey...!"

I think it's a pity to see the whole series go down the drain. Of course, we can't go back to the old characterisation now. We need something more sophisticated, a character which suggests a certain psychological insight; and this, I suppose, is what Canon Montefiore is attempting to provide. We also need some sort of recognition of the moral ambivalence you'd expect in a god, and of the essentially illusory nature of power.

My advice to the company is to get the theologians off the programme. No theologian ever wrote a good legend.

A Wisp of Azure

My Bank Holiday was sombrely illumined by Miss Freya Stark's long essay in *The Times*, entitled "The qualities needed to escape from mediocrity." Miss Stark's analysis of the nation's situation is bold and outspoken: we're decadent.

"The decadence is there," she argues, "and anyone can spot it, from a lack of candour in public life to the fact that scarce a clock in any London street now tells the time correctly—from right and left in chaos to eccentricities of dress."

A solidly documented case, certainly—the wrongness of the clocks is a particularly damning piece of evidence. The conclusion came as no surprise to me. So far as I know, human society has been in a state of perpetual decadence ever since writers first discovered how to spell the word, and the chances that we might somehow have slipped into a state of undecadence since the publication of the last indictment seemed fairly slim, even before the Bank Holiday.

What strikes me most forcefully about Miss Stark's arguments is the prose they're expressed in, which is largely verse—a rare quality for prose to possess in this decadent age, and one which the compositors at *The Times* seem to have overlooked in laying the piece out.

Take the passage I quoted. "The de/cadence/ is there,/ and an/yone/ can spot it," she starts off, in five iambs and an amphibrach. The lack of candour in public life seems to have defeated her powers of metrification, as well it might, but she comes back strongly, in iambs varied with the occasional amphibrach again, on the fact

> *That scarce a clock in any London street*
> *Now tells the time correctly—*
> *From right and left in chaos*
> *To eccentricities of dress.*

She concedes that many of these symptoms "are straws/ that an/y wind/ might carry." What forms and phenomena the children of a particular age deck themselves with, she admits, is

> *Like foam dissolving on waves that dupe themselves*
> *To stabilise the sands of time they cover.*

I'm not too happy about that anapaest at the third foot of the first pentameter, but Shakespeare wouldn't have bothered about the odd anapaest in blank verse, and anyway, in a decadent age like ours you must expect a little rough workmanship here and there. In any case, Miss Stark makes up for it handsomely by *rhyming* a couplet before the end of the paragraph:—

> *Their fluid arabesque need not detain us,*
> *But rather that hidden force beneath it push-*
> *Ing it with sonorous monotony*
> *Ashore. What power lifts it with such pulsations,*
> *Such raising and lowering of nations.*
> *Which we call progress and decay?*

The question here is not rhetorical, for it turns out that the power which lifts the fluid arabesque, with such pulsations, and, indeed, such raising and lowering of nations, is (or are) two fallacies. There's nothing like a couple of fallacies if you've got an arabesque to lift.

The fallacies in question, which Miss Stark believes gained currency after the First World War, are that mediocrity can lead to, or substitute for, Excellence. Miss Stark does not totally dismiss mediocrity, in spite of its small "m"; she calls it, among other things,

> *The golden mean, the weft and woof of habit,*
> *The vine and fig tree of Isaiah . . .*

But she prefers Excellence, with a capital "E," which she describes as a "sprite," and "not a result, but an apparition." She says it "comes out of the deep well and is either reached by its own paths or not at all." And she writes:—

> *It is whatever life may mean*
> *Apart from daily living,*
> *A wisp of azure,*
> *A visitation to the mind or heart.*

The trouble is, apparently, that instead of lifting up our eyes to the hills and dreaming dreams, we rested on our oars in a victorious sunset. So now mediocrity "creeps into our English garden, where Shakespeare is still not only read but enjoyed, by a simple act of carpentry, the setting-up of the bed of Procrustes." (Is it the reading or the creeping which is done by carpentry? An ingenious bit of carpentry, in either case.) But what of the future? Miss Stark drops into tetrameters:—

It would be desperate to watch
Our hemisphere rolling into night
Without a certainty of dawn,
And day will come, we may be sure....

Yet not/ so safe/ly sure, she warns, that "our own people will carry its banner." It's all up to the young.

Youth must think hard, and may walk free.
Its feet on a mediocre and
Perhaps improving floor,
But its head as high as may be in the clouds.

A hopeful note to end her sombre tale. But yet it seems to me that youth may fail, while keeping wrapped in cloud his thoughtful head, that mediocre floor to safely tread. And if the floor in mediocre manner his stumbling feet should once betray, he might put out his hand and drop the *banner*, with which he beckons on the approaching *day*.

If no day dawns, no *azure wisp* can light the clouds which do the youthful face benight. Without a wisp, how can the lad unscrew or otherwise the *carpentry* undo? But with the carpentry still firmly screwed, he'll miss the private *path* into the *well*, where not *results* but *apparitions* brood, and where the *sprite* herself is known to dwell.

And if we haven't got the blasted sprite, we'll *never* get those damned clocks running right.

What the Stars Foretell

It's odd how the Guide Michelin has established itself in English mythology. Few British tourists, hammering across France with a carload of camping equipment and the last £10 traveller's cheque preserved next to their heart, can afford anything more than the most modest of restaurants. Yet each new edition of the Guide is scrutinised by British newspapers, as if it were "Who's Who" or the Honours List, for new accessions to three-star status, or even more interesting, demotions therefrom. And when the proprietors of demoted three-star restaurants shoot themselves, that shows the French behaving in an even more amusingly French way still.

Like Inspector Maigret and the *police judiciaire*, the team of Michelin agents who eat their way so secretly, expertly, and high-mindedly around France have caught the English imagination. One day there will be an English television series featuring Patrick Wymark as *l'inspecteur* Finbec of the Service Michelin (the Ser' Mich', as they call it in the business), one of the dedicated, lonely men who drive the long straight roads of France in their dark Peugeots (disguised with Pirelli tyres), grimly hunting down over-cooked artichokes in small country towns filled with birdsong.

In the first instalment, Finbec has scarcely finished his *salade niçoise* in a little restaurant in Cahiers (Marne-et-Loire), when the *patronne* says that her husband is away, and that she has some *primeurs* of asparagus upstairs in her room....

I think it's a pity that the mythology of the red Michelin has eclipsed that of the other famous Michelin guides—the *guides verts*. The green guides are the regional touring ones, and marvellous guides they are, with intelligent information about industry, geology, and the events of the last war, as well as old churches.

The *guides verts* have their own system of star-grading, with which they classify the attractions of towns, villages, beauty spots, public monuments, and works of art. Three stars means "worth a journey"; two stars—"worth a detour"; one— "interesting." Then there are two lower categories, distinguished only by the size of the type-face on the maps—places which are "to be seen if the occasion arises," and "reference-points," which aren't to be seen even if the occasion does arise, but merely used to find the way to more fortunate locations.

So presumably there is an even larger force of green Michelin inspectors driving the roads of France in their discreet Peugeots, anonymously assessing the merits of abbey, view, and public fountain. Inspectors in the *Mich' vert* division of the service rather look down on those in the *Mich' rouge*, I suspect. Something of the branch's traditions comes through in this quietly dramatic report sent back to head office by *l'inspecteur* (*vert*) Pondéré after his triennial inspection of Grince (Charente-et-Oise)★★★.

"The speciality of Grince is its *cathédrale gothique avec le beffroi à la mode de Rouen*. But when I arrived (at 4.30 p.m.) I was informed by a rather surly verger, wearing a cassock which was none too clean, that the visit to the belfry was off. So was the visit to the treasury, and I had to make do with a cold and under-lighted crypt.

"I hoped I might have better luck with the *bas-reliefs en marbre de St-Boisson*, but they turned out to be undergoing repair and half-hidden behind screens. I washed the *cathédrale* down with a promising-looking *Chateau de Montvizier* 1542, which turned out to be reasonably viewable, though somewhat lacking in body and mellowness.

"I rounded the occasion off by sampling Grince's much-praised *panorama du belvédère de St-Astuce sur la vallée de la Buze*, to which we awarded three stars in our last edition. I regret to report that I found a large cement factory floating in the middle of the view, which entirely destroyed my appetite for it.

"I recommend that Grince should be reclassified 'to be seen if the occasion arises.' "

When this alarming report reaches headquarters, of course, a gigantic intelligence operation is put into motion. A whole team of secret agents infiltrates Grince and the surrounding countryside to check Pondéré's assessment. Every aspect of the town's Principal Curiosities and Other Curiosities is probed and sifted.

And when the Awards Committee sits down to consider the case, the whole field of comparative beauty-spot aesthetics comes under review. Are Gothic cathedrals perhaps a somewhat overrated form of architectural expression altogether? On the other hand, does a cement factory really spoil the view? Isn't there a case for saying that a cement factory, and a landscape whitened by cement dust, is a more characteristic expression of the twentieth century than old-fashioned woods and cornfields?

And is the Finger of St-Bolophon, which wags at pilgrims from its reliquary in Grince Cathedral on the third Sunday of

April, before the tourist season starts, really more delightful than the Bile of Ste-Théodosie at Le Hoquet, which liquefies on the second Sunday of August, when the season is at its height?

The whole subject is so complex, and the general principles so hotly disputed, that the Committee decides to leave Grince with one of its stars as a compromise. Even so, of course, when the new edition of the guide appears the Mayor of Grince poisons himself and the Bishop flees to South America.

But, in the British papers, not a word.

East of Suez

An extract from the signal log of HMS Ubiquitous, on passage in the Indian Ocean.

C-in-C Singapore to Ubiquitous: Urgent amendment sailing orders. Courtesy call South African ports cancelled. Re-embark all coloured personnel and Chinese cooks debarked in anticipation SA visit and alter course forthwith for Aden. Render all necessary assistance required by local civil and military authorities to maintain order during disturbances.

Report position and estimated time of arrival Aden.

Ubiquitous to C-in-C Singapore: Your signal received and understood. Wilco. My position 3.15 N 79.44 E. Estimated time of arrival Aden—early June.

C-in-C Singapore to Ubiquitous: Cancel my last signal. Re-debark Chinese cooks and proceed with all possible speed Hong Kong make show of strength during civil disturbances. Equip shore patrols with anti-riot weapons. Stand by to take over Hong Kong–Kowloon ferry service from strikers.

Report position and ETA Hong Kong.

Ubiquitous to C-in-C Singapore: Wilco. Have fetched round to take up easterly course and my position is once again 3.15 N 79.44 E. ETA Hong Kong—Tuesday week.

C-in-C Singapore to Ubiquitous: Most urgent. Abandon course Hong Kong and make all possible speed Gulf of Aqaba. Stand by southern approaches to Strait of Tiran outside territorial waters establishing British presence but in view delicate situation in area establish it with maximum circumspection. Report position and ETA Tiran.

Ubiquitous to C-in-C Singapore: Wilco. Have come round on to westerly course again and am back at 3.15 N 79.44 E. ETA Tiran—mid-June.

C-in-C Singapore to Ubiquitous: Note amendment previous signal. In view local customs and feelings debark Jewish personnel before proceeding Tiran.

Ubiquitous to C-in-C Singapore: Wilco. In view possible Papal pronouncement on situation advise whether should keep RCs below decks.

C-in-C Singapore to Ubiquitous: Urgent amendment previous signals. Re-embark forthwith all Jewish personnel debark coloured personnel and proceed with maximum dispatch Macao. Establish British presence outside territorial waters in support British consul. Report ETA Macao.

Ubiquitous to C-in-C Singapore: Wilco. ETA Macao uncertain but expect to be back at 3.15 N 79.44 E in approximately 10 minutes.

C-in-C Singapore to Ubiquitous: Urgent re-amendment to amended orders. Political situation United Nations re Aqaba question makes immediate courtesy call African port essential. Debark all white personnel and proceed forthwith Mombasa.

Ubiquitous to C-in-C Singapore: Wilco. Advise whether Chinese cooks classified white or coloured in Mombasa.

C-in-C Singapore to Ubiquitous: Correction. Proceed Shanghai establish discreet British presence in support two British diplomats being glued by crowd. In view local sensibilities re defectors re-debark Chinese cooks again.

Ubiquitous to C-in-C Singapore: Wilco.

C-in-C Singapore to Ubiquitous: Cancel last signal. Proceed at once Gibraltar make discreet show of strength outside territorial waters off Algeciras.

Ubiquitous to C-in-C Singapore: Show of strength imposs-ible without full complement Chinese cooks.

C-in-C Singapore to Ubiquitous: Re-re-embark Chinese cooks forthwith. Astonished not re-embarked already.

Ubiquitous to C-in-C Singapore: Wilco. Advise whether should circumnavigate world eastabout or westabout.

C-in-C Singapore to Ubiquitous: Westabout calling at Malta for major refit. Imperative you reassure local population HM Government still using base.

Ubiquitous to C-in-C Singapore: Wilco. Have kept helm hard over and am almost back at 3.15 N 79.44 E again.

C-in-C Singapore to Ubiquitous: Correction. Proceed eastabout via North-West Passage so as pass Iceland protect British trawlers suffering harassment Icelandic gunboats.

Ubiquitous to C-in-C Singapore: Wilco.

C-in-C Singapore to Ubiquitous: Your signal very faint.

Ubiquitous to C-in-C Singapore: My signalman very dizzy. But British presence at 3.15 N 79.44 E almost overpowering. Situation here entirely under control.

C-in-C Singapore to Ubiquitous: Well done Ubiquitous. But in view general world feeling debark all personnel with British nationality before proceeding further.

Private Collections

I wish people weren't so coy about showing their slides and films and snapshots. You have to drag the stuff out of them, as though it were their first efforts at poetry.

They let themselves be frightened off by the convention that one's snaps are boring to others. But the truth is more or less the opposite. It's oneself who is likely to be bored, since one has seen it all before; to others they're almost certainly fascinating.

At any rate, they are to me, in any reasonable moderation. I find the prospect of sorting a huge muddled parcel of somebody else's snapshots over the carpet on a winter's afternoon, or of sitting in the calm after-dinner darkness watching the brilliantly coloured images of someone else's life succeed one another on the screen, a distinctly cheering one.

I don't mean so much the pictures of the Baptistry at Pisa, or the barefoot boy driving goats on Naxos, or the Hopi initiation ceremony in New Mexico (though I must admit I enjoy these too). I mean the really basic stuff—the pictures taken by our old friend Horace Morris of his wife Doris, with the sun in her eyes and a telegraph pole growing out of her head; the pictures of Horace by Doris where he is striking a humorous attitude on top of a rock, with his feet bigger than his head, half his head missing, and the horizon at 10 degrees to the horizontal.

I suppose it's partly plain curiosity about how other people live their lives when one's not around to watch. But there's more to it than that. I think one is perhaps soothed to have some nagging unconscious solipsism stilled by this evidence of the world's independent existence.

"The mystical thing," wrote Wittgenstein in the *Tractatus*, "is not *how* the world is, but *that* it is." And since the arrangement of things in these pictures is unimportant, we are brought face to face with this fundamental aspect—the sheer fact that there was a moment in the history of the world when Doris Morris stood in front of a telegraph pole, and screwed up her eyes against the sun; that whatever was or was not, a rock with Horace Morris on top of it was.

The moment has gone. The state of affairs that united Horace and rock has disappeared beneath a thousand million succeeding states of affairs, and minute by minute grows remoter still. Horace will become too old to climb upon rocks; the rock will be worn down to sand by the sea; the photograph itself will fade and disintegrate. But nothing will ever destroy the fact it recorded for long enough to be appreciated—that at one particular moment this one particular state of affairs did obtain.

I suppose newspaper photographs and television images say no less. But I suspect that we don't entirely believe them. We accept them, as we do the accounts given by physicists of molecular structure, but we don't intimately feel the reality of them, as we do of the things which touch upon our own existence and identity. If we registered all those pictures of suffering, wealth, and action as anything more than a sort of factual fairyland, they would overwhelm us.

But poor old Horace Morris I *know*. My total belief in his reality might falter if I saw him on television, discussing the country's economic situation. But to the top of that only too probable rock, to a position 10 degrees out of the vertical, with too much foot and too little head, my belief will follow him unquestioningly.

And on, by extension, beyond him, to the world outside the frame of the picture. To the cigarette packet lying half-buried in the sand, just seven feet to the right. To the two men who walked by, three minutes earlier, gazing down at the sand as they talked, the one absently swinging at pieces of seaweed with a child's plastic spade, while the other gestured with his right hand, and said, "That may be so, I don't dispute that for a moment, it may very well be so, I wouldn't argue with you on that. . . ." To the faint drone of aircraft passing high overhead, on their way out from that particular time and place to other countries, other days.

I like the modesty of snapshots—the fact that they make no claims, imply no principles, demand no reactions. They don't, like news photographs, claim to show anything typical, or illustrative, of matters outside themselves. They don't, like advertising pictures, attempt to suggest attitudes or courses of action.

They make a counterpoise to art, too. For the convention of all art is that things can be arranged, or selected, or lighted, or simplified, or emphasised, to bring out some significance within or beyond the objects themselves; or that events can be represented as falling out in such a way that they cast some special illumination upon human behaviour; or that men can be driven by the pressure of extreme circumstances to some special self-knowledge or self-revelation.

One accepts this as the convention which makes art possible. But so universal is it that it comes to seem more like a natural law. And what *that* suggests is that there really is, in the external world, some special "truth" which the everyday appearance of things conceals; and that the real significance of these appearances is that they can be manipulated by the artist to reveal this truth.

The snapshot, however, reminds us that the world is not like this—that things are what they are, and that they are significant in themselves, for their own sake. Horace Morris, on his rock, stands for nothing, except Horace Morris on a rock; typifies nothing, except Horace Morris on a rock; purports to reveal no truth about the nature of Horace Morris or the rock, except that at this particular moment of time the one was standing on the other, and that together they looked thus and so.

Horace for Horace's sake—a good working principle.

Save it for the Stairs

Esprit de l'escalier is a maddening form of cerebral activity; but *politesse de l'escalier* is a good deal worse. I'm an expert on all branches of the subject; I think of pretty well everything in life, from witty replies to fundamental moral attitudes, only afterwards, on the way downstairs, and it's the belated realisation of my failure to have made the appropriate polite remarks which casts me into the greatest despair of all.

It's not only on *escaliers* that the point comes sickeningly home to one, of course, but in the *rue*, the *bain*, and perhaps most frequently of all, in the *lit*, in the *milieu* of the *nuit*. Suddenly the faulty connection sparks, and a dismal shock goes through one. Oh, God—one never asked O. J. Sprout how his poor wife was! Holy heaven—one never thanked Christopher and Lavinia Crumble for putting one in touch with that marvellous little man of theirs in Market Strayborough! One never congratulated Thorsten Trouncer on the birth of his son! Never asked Diminua Pinn if she'd got that job she was up for! Never evinced any surprise or pleasure to see Mrs. Haddock out of hospital again!

And once more it's borne in upon one what an insufferable egotist one is—indifferent to other people's triumphs and sufferings, forgetful of their kindness as soon as one has made use of it. How hurt all those poor souls must have felt, as they struggled bravely to smile and talk about politics, when all they really wanted was to hear some passing word of interest in the size of their family, some grudging expression of sympathy on the state of their pancreas!

Except, of course, that they almost certainly wanted nothing of the sort.

Because the odd truth about the expression of polite interest—impossible as this is to believe when one has failed to offer it—is that people really *don't* want to be on the receiving end of it. It's not pleasing but irritating to have to explain for the twentieth time why one's hand is in bandages; not gratifying but embarrassing to announce for the thirtieth time that one got the job, or the prize, or the nomination; and not soothing but humiliating to have to report, for the fortieth time, that one failed to. Pregnancy is a great condition for attracting polite interest, various women have told me. They have sometimes felt, they said, that if one more kindly inquirer asked politely when the baby was due they would fall into screaming hysterics and give birth on the spot.

In fact, as modern politeness analysis shows, the principal—and often the only—beneficiary from the expression of polite interest is the interest-taker, and not the subject of the interest at all. The subject is merely being exploited to increase the interest-taker's sense of psychosocial well-being. Or so some of us at the Self-Justification Research Centre feel.

Let us examine a typical case in our records. "James," a chronically inadequate interest-taker, has been subject since childhood to *politesse de l'escalier* and subsequent bouts of remorse. In a recurring situation, he finds himself up against "Oscar," a skilled and relentless interest-taker with deeply sympathetic eyes and a forehead already wrinkled with altruistic anxiety. The following typical encounter makes it fairly clear which of them it is who is gaining the greater psychosocial profit from the relationship.

"Are you feeling better?" asks Oscar as soon as they meet, with a specially solicitous smile.

"Better?" queries James nervously. "Better than what?"

"Better than you were last time we met. You had a dreadful cold, if you remember."

"Oh, did I?"

"Oh, a terrible one. You still look a tiny bit under the weather, as a matter of fact. How do you feel?"

James starts to explain that he does have a slight but tiresome catarrh, and is still coughing a little. Oscar nods earnestly, evidently appalled by every symptom. Then suddenly James's tone becomes a little uncertain. He has just been struck, as any competent politeness analyst would realise immediately, by the faint but troubling recollection that Oscar himself is a martyr to some very serious and painful disease.

But before he can remember exactly what it is, Oscar is asking him how he enjoyed his recent trip to Boulogne. James holds forth at some length on the amusing ubiquity of English fish and chips in the town, etc., etc.—when suddenly the anecdotes falter, and a strained look comes over his face. The uneasy suspicion has just come to him, as we politeness analysts see at once, that Oscar has just got back from Peru. Or is just off to Peking. Or was born and brought up in Boulogne. Or....

But already Oscar is asking if James's son enjoyed his birthday the previous week. Open alarm seizes James. Does this mean that Oscar sent a present, he thinks, and that I'm supposed to thank him for it? Did I send his child a present on its birthday? Does he *have* children?

"And that reminds me," says Oscar, his brow wrinkling anxiously once more. "How is Deirdre, your second cousin once removed? Has she recovered from that rather nasty fall she had the year before last?"

James mumbles in incoherent consternation. What fall? What second cousin once removed? How does Oscar know more about his family than he does himself?

"You were telling me about it," says Oscar helpfully, "when

you came to dinner last (and I really must thank you once again for your kindness in coming). Remember?"

Almost certainly not. But he will, Oscar, he will. On the *escalier* afterwards. Together with the fact that you got a Nobel Prize last week, are just about to swim the Atlantic single-handed, and have still not had back the dinner-jacket, the electric drill, and the copy of "Finnegans Wake" you lent him.

But it's James, as we at the Self-Justification Research Centre believe, who will go to heaven.

A Very Special Collection

I had a letter the other day from the Mugar Memorial Library at Boston University, kindly inviting me to send them my manuscripts and correspondence files, so that they could be "curated under optimum archival conditions" in a special "Michael Frayn Collection."

I declined this unexpected honour, for reasons which seemed cogent enough at the time. Now, in silent reproach, the library has sent me a lavishly illustrated brochure about their Special Collections—their "jewelled showcase," as they call them—and I realise what a fool I was.

Just to think—by now the precious papers could be inside an acid-free envelope in a humidity-controlled vault, on the sixth floor of a building to which "Modern Baroque architecture has given a special opulence," instead of on the floor at home being drawn on by the children. They could be taking their turn for revolving display in the exhibition hall, which is framed, as the brochure explains, by a picture window "draped grey in translucent yarn to give a sense rather than sight of the trolley-infested street outside," and whose rooms are divided by glass walls "allowing floor surfaces to flow into each, conspiring for spatial illusion and playing with the magic of light."

The library houses what the brochure claims to be probably the largest collection of its sort in America, with contributors ranging alphabetically from Eric Ambler, "through torch singer Libby Holman," to Alec Waugh. Leslie Charteris is in. So is Ngaio Marsh, and the manuscript of "Born Free."

There's not space in the brochure to illustrate all these riches, of course, but they do have a page from one of their real treasures—the typescript of "Rally Round the Flag, Boys!" by Max Shulman, which makes the value of this sort of collection abundantly clear.

As readers of Shulman will no doubt recall, he describes the life of his character Guido as being "singularly free of vicissitudes." But this is not what Shulman originally wrote! He described it initially as "singularly free *from* vicissitudes." Then, upon mature reflection, he changed it. "Free from" to "free of"; here we have a first-hand picture of the writer at work.

The brochure also contains the facsimile of a page from "Fantastic Voyage," by Isaac Asimov, based upon a screenplay by Harry Kleiner, which in turn was based upon an original story by Otto Klement and Jay Lewis Bixby. This is another extraordinarily revealing document. For one thing, Asimov types much worse than Shulman. Better than me, but worse than Shulman. That helps to place him, I think.

And the revisions he's made! There's enough material for a thesis in this one page alone! "Grant nodded," he typed curtly for a start (p. 94, line 14). Then he crossed out "nodded," and inserted "continued to stare about in wonder." You see? The whole character of Grant has changed. The neutral, merely acquiescent Grant of Harry Kleiner's conception, not to mention Otto Klement's and Jay Lewis Bixby's, has matured through Asimov's rich reworking into Grant the wonderer, Grant the curious observer, Grant the *concerned*—in a word, Grant as he has come down to us today.

The brochure illustrates a composition by Bizet, transcribed and written out by one of the *actual composer's actual contemporaries!* There is a post-card from George Bernard Shaw (*the* George Bernard Shaw) to Claude Rains (*the* Claude Rains), directing him to change two lines in "Caesar and Cleopatra." The brochure illustrates not only the message side of the card, but also the address side. It contains the address of Claude Rains, interestingly enough. And a postage stamp.

And here's a scoop—an actual Christmas card sent by John F. Kennedy and his wife to Gladys Hasty Carroll! "Wishing you a Blessed Christmas and a New Year filled with happiness, Senator and Mrs. John F. Kennedy," reads the printed text, followed by the autograph, "Best—Jack." "Best" is spelt "B-E-S-T."

But manuscript is not the only commodity they're curating out there. The Henry Roth Collection includes a mailbox, through which most of the correspondence between Roth and his publishers apparently passed. The mailbox is pictured in the brochure; it carries the autograph "Roth" on its side in roughly painted capitals, and the lid doesn't close properly.

Looking at it, you can imagine Roth (embittered, according to the text, by the tepid public response to his book "Call It Sleep") going out into the storm to collect the latest depressing news from his publishers. He is embittered still further to find the rain has got in through the open lid, turning the wad of circulars from the local supermarkets into a sodden pulp, and thereby gravely prejudicing their value as historico-literary documents—you can see it all! Lord, the life we writers lead!

They are also curating Anthony Newley's hat in the Anthony Newley Collection. I'm thinking of applying for a research grant to go and study it. I'd like to see it *in situ*—nestling in its acid-free hatbox in the humidity-controlled vaults, or framed by the picture-window with the trolley-infested street beyond, and surrounded by the conspiracy of spatial illusion and the magic play of light.

In the meantime I think I'd better send them a pair or two of my old socks, so that they can start the Michael Frayn Collection after all. I'll throw in a birthday card from my Great-Uncle Alexander, and part of the cardboard box I keep my old bank statements in, signed "Crosse and Blackwell."

I hate to see the stuff go out of the country, of course. But when scholarship calls, the dustman must take second place.